Elinor Ostro.

Elinor Ostrom's Rules for Radicals

Cooperative Alternatives Beyond Markets and States

Derek Wall

PLUTO PRESS

First published 2017 by Pluto Press
345 Archway Road, London N6 5AA

www.plutobooks.com

British Library Cataloguing in Publication Data
A catalogue record for this book is available from the British Library

ISBN   978 0 7453 9936 2   Hardback
ISBN   978 0 7453 9935 5   Paperback
ISBN   978 1 7868 0122 7   PDF eBook
ISBN   978 1 7868 0124 1   Kindle eBook
ISBN   978 1 7868 0123 4   EPUB eBook

This book is printed on paper suitable for recycling and made from fully
managed and sustained forest sources. Logging, pulping and manufacturing
processes are expected to conform to the environmental standards of the
country of origin.

Typeset by Stanford DTP Services, Northampton, England

Simultaneously printed in the United Kingdom and United States of America

Contents

To Estella Schmid

Acknowledgements

On the two occasions when I briefly met Elinor Ostrom, she was open, enthusiastic (despite her ill health) and answered my questions with patience. Her thoughts and actions continue to inspire me and give me hope. My wife Emily Blyth read every word of my text, made numerous suggestions and supported me in this project. The mistakes are all mine, the positive effects this text produces are the product of the practical labour of Elinor and Emily.

Of the many individuals who read drafts and made suggestions I would like in particular to thank Romayne Phoenix for her enthusiasm.

Political economy students in the Department of Politics, Goldsmiths College, University of London are familiar with Ostrom's work, I must thank them for their keen interest and thank my colleague Paul Gunn for his enthusiastic inclusion of her work in his teaching. My 2016/17 cohort of New Radical Political Economy students were able to argue vigorously but respectfully with each other with opposing views on Marxist and Austrian economics, Elinor would have loved their passionate contestations and engagement with her work.

So many others made this project happen. David Castle was a patient editor. Anna Heyman also made useful suggestions to improve the book.

I was doing a bunch of research through the years that many people thought was very radical and people didn't like. As a person who does interdisciplinary work, I didn't fit anywhere. I was relieved that, after all these years of struggle, someone really thought it did add up. That's very nice.

—Elinor Ostrom,
interview with Fran Korten in 2010 (Korten 2010)

Rules for Radicals

1. Think about institutions
2. Pose social change as problem solving
3. Embrace diversity
4. Be specific
5. Listen to the people
6. Self-government is possible
7. Everything changes
8. Map power
9. Collective ownership can work
10. Human beings are part of nature too
11. All institutions are constructed, so can be constructed differently
12. No panaceas
13. Complexity does not mean chaos.

1

Elinor Ostrom's Radical Life

[A] core goal of public policy should be to facilitate the development
of institutions that bring out the best in humans.

(Ostrom and Ostrom 2014: 197)

Elinor Ostrom (1933–2012) was the first and, as I write, so far the
only woman to win a Nobel Prize for economics. Strictly speaking
there isn't a Nobel Prize for economics, but the Riksbank Prize in
Economic Sciences in Memory of Alfred Nobel, which Ostrom
shared with another institutional economist, Oliver Williamson. She
won the award, according to the Nobel Committee 'for her analysis
of economic governance, especially the commons', and is best known
for her book *Governing the Commons* (1990). So, what is meant by
the commons and why are they a subject of interest?

Commons are collective forms of ownership. In Britain, commons
often take the form of land which is open to members of a community
to graze livestock, fly kites or walk upon. An example that I am familiar
with and often have the pleasure of visiting, because it is relatively
local to me, is Cricklade North Meadow. North Meadow, near
Swindon in the English county of Wiltshire, is one of the UK's most
important wildlife sites. It is famous for beautiful flowers including
the rare snake's head fritillary. The meadow has been maintained as
a commons since before the Norman conquest of 1066. As it is the
commons I am most familiar with it will be discussed as an example
at various points in this text. Fisheries and forests may be commons,
and the concept as a legal form has been extended to free software
and the World Wide Web. The biologist Garrett Hardin wrote 'The
Tragedy of the Commons' in 1968, arguing that collective property
was inevitably doomed to failure, because it would be abused by users
(Hardin 1968). For example, too many cattle would be placed on the
village green and it would be over grazed. The tragedy is that if no

one individual privately owns a resource such as a field, people tend to exploit the good nature of others, fail to look after it and eventually it is wrecked. Or at least this is what Hardin argued. Yet increasingly, commons have been seen, on the left as a form of social collective ownership, perhaps even the basis for a communism (Hardt 2010).

Elinor Ostrom won the Nobel for 'demonstrating how local property can be successfully managed by local commons without any regulation by central authorities or privatization' (Nobel.org 2009). She argued that commons, including common land, forests or fisheries that were owned collectively, could be conserved. This was radical stuff; other economists argued, along with Garrett Hardin, that collective ownership would always fail because of the 'tragedy of the commons' which led to over use and disaster. However, she was not a leftist in a traditional sense and did not see commons as a straightforward alternative to private ownership in all circumstances.

According to Ostrom indigenous people and others have often maintained commons for hundreds or even thousands of years without destroying these environments. Ostrom argued that democratic control, rather than top-down management or simple privatisation, works to conserve nature. She can be seen as an ecological thinker, an advocate of cooperation and a subverter of economic notions of purely private ownership. This chapter provides a brief biography before discussing her potential contributions to radical political, economic and social transformation.

ELINOR OSTROM

Elinor was born in 1933 in Los Angeles, California, the daughter of Adrian and Leah Awan. Leah was originally a musician from South Dakota. Adrian was a set designer who worked for the Hollywood Bowl and Civic Light Opera, among other projects. Her parents divorced when she was a child. Her early years, shaped by divorce, the depression and the Second World War, seem to have instilled a frugality in her that is perhaps unusual for economists and might have contributed to her later passion for ecological living. She helped in the garden and with canning fruit produced by her mother. She felt that part of the solution to environmental problems would come with us consuming less and downsizing.

She saw her first step on the road to the commons as occurring when she became at student at Beverly Hills High School. Beverly Hills High School is well known for its students who went on to become Hollywood film directors and actors. Elinor felt that it was an accident of geography that she attended the school. In turn, the school promoted academic achievement; without attending Beverly Hills it is unlikely that she would have gone to university,

'Technically, we lived in Los Angeles, but the high school was literally across the street,' she said. 'I'm very grateful for that opportunity, because 90 percent of the kids who went to Beverly Hills High School went on to college. I don't think I would have gone to college if not for being in that environment'. (Leonard 2009)

She suffered from a stutter and was encouraged to join first the poetry society and then the debating society, supposedly to help her with this problem. The debating society promoted both an interest in politics and mental flexibility derived from the fact that she would often have to debate one side of an argument before then arguing the case against. She completed high school in 1951 and went to study politics at University of California Los Angeles, where she graduated in 1954. She married a fellow UCLA student Charles Scott and moved with him to Boston. Charles studied law at Harvard and she worked in personnel departments to fund him. "'Basically I put my husband through law school and he entered a corporate law firm," she said. "I was thinking of doing a PhD, and he was not too enthusiastic"' (Leonard 2009). They divorced, but it seems to have been a relatively amicable break up. "'That's problem solving, too," she observed. "Sometimes, with couples, it's OK to say it's not working and it's not going to work and you move on"' (ibid.).

In deciding to pursue an academic career, she believed that economics was an obvious choice. Some of her work towards her politics degree was in the form of economics units, and she had enjoyed and excelled in them. Sadly, she was prevented from taking economics because it was claimed she had not studied enough mathematics at high school. In turn, at school when she had asked to study further mathematics this had been refused because she was a woman! Her school advisor, she claimed, had asked what use trigonometry would be when she was 'barefoot and pregnant in the kitchen' (Cronin 2012: 90).

Even carrying out her second choice of a politics PhD proved controversial:

> Surprisingly, the Financial Aid Committee awarded four assistant-ships to women that year after 40 years without a woman on the faculty or as a PhD student. The four of us learned mid-semester that this decision had been strongly criticized at a faculty meeting. Some faculty members were concerned that allocating four out of 40 assistantships to women was a waste of departmental resources. They feared that none of us would obtain good academic positions, which would harm the department's reputation. Fortunately, fellow graduate students encouraged the four of us to ignore the concerns of the faculty who opposed our appointments. They also advised us whom to stay away from during our graduate program if we could. (Ostrom 2010b: 3)

Elinor found that much of the political theory she was taught, typically dealing with figures such as Hobbes, Machiavelli and Rousseau covered the biographies of such important thinkers but did not lead to a clear accumulation of knowledge. She was frustrated because she felt that political science did not attempt to build analysis in a step by step way, but focused on personalities and conflicting schools of thought. To her it was as if biology was continuing to debate Lamarck and Darwin, focusing on their lives, loves and dis-agreements, rather than gaining an understanding of the natural world from their work. She found more inspiration from Vincent Ostrom, whose seminars she attended. It seems to have been love at first sight and they married in 1965.

Vincent was born in Nooksack, Washington on 25 September 1919 (New 2012). His parents were recent immigrants from Jamatland in Sweden and the name Ostrom means 'island in the river'. The

Ostroms farmed mink, and for Vincent conservation and farming were a lifelong fascination. He studied politics at UCLA, teaching in Ontario, California and gaining his PhD in 1950. His academic work linked local government, economics, ecology, game theory and much else, he was a multidimensional thinker. He was passionate about medieval city states, indigenous politics, the origins of the US constitution, the African revolutionary Amílcar Cabral and deep democracy based on self-government rather than state action. He was fascinated by how farmers managed their land and cooperated with each other to solve practical environmental problems. He was also intrigued by how language and culture shaped politics including our relationship with the environment. It would over simplify his work to say that he was an anarchist but he saw politics as something beyond formal governments and political parties.

When I met Elinor Ostrom in 2012, shortly before she died, she insisted that Vincent had been interested in commons long before meeting her. When he died just days after her, his inspiration for her work was noted:

In 1943, while earning his M.A., Vincent began teaching at Chaffey Union High School in Ontario, Calif. It was here that he made observations that not only created a foundation for his master's thesis, but also the work his wife would later dedicate her career to.

During the two years he taught in Ontario, Vincent noticed that citrus-growing smallholders created a system of land and water rights that provided what the farmers needed to sustain the farms' incomes. The community also created an endowment for the local high school and a planned college.

In short, he realized that a group of people with common interests and needs could create their own systems and institutions to achieve complex objectives – without any outside governance. (New 2012)

Whereas Garrett Hardin talked about the tragedy of the commons, Vincent had studied the management of common pool resources and collective environmental management with care. His interest in ground water basins dealt with a classic potential tragedy of the commons, and one of his early books was entitled simply *Water and Politics* (V. Ostrom 1953). His PhD examined the theme of 'Government and Water: A Study of the Influence of Water upon Governmental Institutions and Practices in the Development of Los Angeles'. He was very much a political ecologist from his early academic work in the 1940s, long before the term 'green politics' had been invented. In 1960 he was approached by both the Kennedy and Nixon presidential campaign teams to draft their environmental policy platform. He chose the Democrats simply because they asked him first (Walljasper 2014).

At his suggestion Elinor studied West Basin, a water source underlying Los Angeles.

> My assignment was the West Basin, which underlay a portion of the city of Los Angeles and 11 other cities. During the first half of the twentieth century, water producers ignored the facts that the level of groundwater underlying Los Angeles was going down and seawater was intruding along the coast. Toward the end of World War II, several municipal water departments asked the U.S. Geological Survey to conduct a major study of the area and agreed to fund one third of the study. The report detailed a grim picture of substantial overdraft and threat of further saltwater intrusion that could eventually ruin the basin for human use. (Ostrom 2010b: 4–5)

If too many users took too much water out of West Basin, it would lower the water level and tend to suck in salt water from the Pacific. Salinization made the water unusable and threatened the whole Basin. Elinor discovered that despite huge difficulties the different users were able to cooperate, ration their extraction of water and maintain the system. They prevented a tragedy of the commons from occurring.

While her academic career eventually wound its way to her Nobel win it was a long and often difficult journey. Elinor completed her PhD and she and Vincent moved to the Bloomington campus of the University of Indiana in 1965. He was appointed as a lecturer and she eventually was given work in the politics department. Initially she had to teach US constitutional politics at 7.30 in the morning, but eventually was able to carry out research and develop her own teaching topics. She developed a research project into policing, arguing that input from local communities led to better policing. This political research was based on anthropology and specifically participant observation; she worked both with African-American citizens and rode in the back of police cars. She began to focus upon governance, local politics and environmental problems. Research visits to what was then West Germany saw her develop an interest in experimental economics and game theory. Her work increasingly focused on commons, and her best known book, *Governing the Commons*, was published in 1990.

ELINOR OSTROM'S RADICAL POLITICAL ECONOMY

Elinor Ostrom may have won a Nobel, or at least shared a Swedish bank prize, for economics, but she was very clear that her discipline was political economy not economics. She saw economics as powerfully shaped by institutions, so in turn saw herself specifically as institutionalist. Institutions are sets of rules created by human beings; economists sometimes forget that economic activity does not just happen, but is shaped by political institutions too.

This emphasis on institutions provides a sophisticated way of viewing economic activity and it is useful for understanding political and social change. She felt that democratic control made for effective problem solving as well as being desirable in its own right, so political institutions needed participation rather than centralised top-down management.

It is my sincere belief, having studied Elinor Ostrom's work with obsessive passion over a period of years and having had the pleasure of meeting her on two occasions, that if human beings are to create a future which is democratic, socially just, equal and, above all, ecologically sustainable, we would do well to examine her arguments with care.

In contrast, some on the left have bluntly argued that her ideas have nothing to offer those of us who seek social change. The Marxist economist Ben Fine suggests that she ignores issues of class struggle and power and, at worst, her work is a form of 'economic colonialism' (Fine 2010). Indeed, while she focused on micro issues, looking at the rules that might be put in place to help or hinder conservation by local communities, she rarely examined the macro issues of why common land might be enclosed and simply taken by more powerful actors including colonisers and corporations. Much of her work appears dry and technical, using the unfamiliar language of game theory, additional formal models and forays into mathematics. While some argue she subverts mainstream economics, Fine contends that she actually applies mainstream market-based economics to new areas, potentially taming the commons with her analysis. It is economic colonialism because it is part of a wider tendency to apply economic logic to non-market areas of human society, such as Becker's analysis of the family or James Buchanan's Public Choice Theory. While I feel that Ostrom would have rejected Becker's work, she drew upon Buchanan and was, at one point, President of the Public Choice Society, normally seen as a right-wing body. Like her good friend Amartya Sen, she seemed to have a paradoxical love–hate relationship with such conservative economists. While a defender of the commons and collective ownership, she was far from being a Marxist or far-left thinker in any conventional sense.

Indeed, Ostrom never claimed to be on the left of politics. She often cited thinkers seen as far from radical, including the conservative economists Friedrich Hayek, Joseph Schumpeter and Frank Knight, and, of course, James Buchanan. She was not a woman who delivered passionate polemics, attended protest marches or involved herself with political parties or social movements. She proudly rejected the notions of utopias, policy manifestos or demands. For a variety of reasons, she seems an unlikely author of a set of rules for radicals.

Yet, despite some caution, I think we can view Ostrom's work as helpful to those on the left seeking positive social change. The French sociologist Pierre Bourdieu argued that 'sociology is a combat sport, a means of self-defense. Basically, you use it to defend yourself, without having the right to use it for unfair attacks' (Bourdieu 2000: 3). While Ostrom was not a sociologist, in the broadest sense she was a social theorist, concerned not only with economics but politics, human psychology, linguistics and the wide culture that is shaped by, and in turn shapes, human behaviour. She developed a body of research that can be used to defend the commons and commoners. Theory, including Ostrom's, can have a material effect. For hundreds of years, perhaps for thousands, collectively-owned resources have been stolen from communities with the simple justification that the commons was inevitably 'tragic'. Left to collective ownership, it is often claimed, individuals would abuse the system and wreck the commons. Either privatisation or strong state control was needed to prevent catastrophe, both alternatives demanded the destruction of the commons and removal of the commoners. While Ostrom felt that there was a possibility that commons could be abused and that this point had to be taken seriously, she argued that this dilemma could be overcome. She found that commons could be made to work and were not automatically doomed because of an intrinsic flaw in human nature. Her careful research is a powerful weapon of self-defence for those who wish to protect a commons under threat.

Equally radical and useful is her notion that economics and politics, potentially, move beyond the market and the state. It is difficult to imagine another economist or even most political economists lecturing on this topic; demand and supply versus government action might appear to be all that we have. On the left we might pay lip service to Marx's notion of the 'withering away of the state' but generally we see either the state or the market. We usually forget that there is more to economics than money or government decisions. The left is often a Keynesian left, agreeing with the economist John Maynard Keynes that markets left to themselves create economic instability and recession, so we need state regulation to make them work better. Marxism, in practice, seems to suggest that central planning is an alternative to the market, rather than promoting Marx's anti-state perspective. Market socialism has become a response for a disillusioned left, who recognise the limits of centralised state-run economies. The argument is that if state socialism fails, more market is needed and if the market fails, more state intervention is desirable. Yet if both fail, what is to be done? The notion that there is something other than the market or the state is apparently unthinkable and is generally unthought of on both the left and the right. Ostrom, in contrast, explicitly saw economics as something that, while including states and markets, could go beyond them. She rather boldly entitled her Nobel lecture 'Beyond Markets and States: Polycentric Governance of Complex Economic Systems' (Ostrom 2010a).

In turn, Elinor Ostrom had an unorthodox and refreshing approach to education and research. Her academic work was based on what she termed co-production, knowledge and theory was constructed with the active participation of the community. She had no time for the kind of academic work that was removed from the population that it sought to study. Her perspective was based not on telling but listening, dethroning academic expertise and asking academics to take note of the people. She believed teamwork was generally more effective than individual work in creating knowledge. She stressed that while she had authored *Governing the Commons* and won an economics prize for doing so, she was part of a larger network. Many of her books and articles were co-authored. She also felt that in researching the commons and allied issues both social and natural science were needed; her interdisciplinary enthusiasm was another reason why she valued team work. Her belief that economics should use qualitative data to understand human behaviour rather than relying on mathematic methods was also far from conventional.

Many of Ostrom's key interests reflect those of an ecosocialist left. If, like me, you are a left-wing member of a Green Party, you will find many of your concerns shared within her work. She focused on ecological sustainability and showed a lifelong commitment to promoting equality. She was an advocate of diversity, celebrating the fact that academic life was beginning to open up to diverse ethnicities and that the status of women in university life was improving. Elinor Ostrom can be seen as moving beyond Eurocentrism, recognising the insights of indigenous people within her work.

She was also radical in that she believed that democracy was key to solving ecological problems and by democracy she meant not just traditional liberal democracy but popular involvement through direct participation, not top-down institutions. She and her husband Vincent spent a lifetime arguing that the more that people were involved in constructing the rules of governance, the better the rules would work. Her inspiration was that of the New England township meeting, where the community made decisions collectively and directly. She thought the exact form that such direct democracy might take was likely to differ from place to place. She also was aware that the township meetings or Athenian assemblies were still limited to a minority, citizenship has to include women, minorities, workers and peasants. Many on the left would see such direct democracy in the Paris Commune, when a revolutionary government of the people governed the city from 18 March to 28 May 1871 before being bloodily put down. But Ostrom, in fact, never (to my knowledge) referred to the Commune or similar socialist forms of deep democracy. This of course reflected her inspiration in either conservative or reformist forms of institutional economics, rather than a literature of revolution.

She was inspired by the French liberal thinker Alexis de Tocqueville. He travelled through the USA in the nineteenth century and wrote his magisterial *Democracy in America*. Here we find his accounts of the township meetings (Tocqueville 1994). Elinor and Vincent Ostrom often referenced *Democracy in America*; it reflected their ideal of participation based on associations made by local people rather than central government.

Vincent wrote that, 'people are presumed, in some meaningful sense, to have self-governing capabilities, such that each mature individual is presumed to be one's own governor, capable of participating in communities of associated relationships and of being knowledgeable about public affairs' (Ostrom 1997: 31). For both Vincent and Elinor, individuals make politics rather than politics being made by just some individuals in a select, supposedly representative elite. They argued that politics runs through society and expands beyond formal structures such as parliaments. The Ostroms also felt that, to the extent that formal politics via political parties, Senates, councils was relevant, it worked best where democracy was deep and participation strong.

There are many paradoxes and contradictions in Elinor's work and indeed in Vincent's. She might be seen as perhaps a conservative thinker and certainly a cautious one if viewed from a particular perspective but as a radical if viewed from another. It's a strange kind of conservatism that sees beyond private property, promotes cooperation and looks to economics that is neither state nor market based.

How do we seek the core of a thinker's ideas? How do we, for Ostrom or any other complex thinker, separate the true from the false? The Dutch philosopher Spinoza grappled with this question in the seventeenth century. Originally a member of the Jewish community in Amsterdam, Spinoza was expelled from his synagogue for unknown heresy. He asked, in his book on religion and politics *Theological-Political Treatise*, how do we decide what is meant by the true religion? (Spinoza 1951). While Spinoza was, on the face of things, discussing religious orthodoxy, he was interested in truth claims in a wider sense. He asked how we could discern the true meaning of a text. The common approach is to argue that there is an essential truth that careful investigation can uncover. We read and criticise and establish the meaning. Spinoza rejected this approach, arguing that texts are written by fallible human beings; even if a religious text is delivered by a deity, we mortals can mishear the holy words. This reminded me of Elinor Ostrom's central question 'How can fallible human beings achieve and sustain self-governing entities and self-governing ways of life as well as sustaining ecological systems?' She posed this to her students; it reflected her work and it reminded me of Spinoza's assumption that we are far from perfect. According to the literary theorist Warren Montag, in a discussion of Spinoza's politics, orthodoxy was empty and the search for an intrinsic core was always false (Montag 1998). Instead one should look at the effects of a text. Spinoza argued that the search for intrinsic and true meaning was used by various religious authorities to gain power over the multitude, but that such a search could be misleading. The meaning of the Bible was in fact very simple: God has only one command which is obedience, obedience specifically to the order that we love our neighbours and promote mutual good. This is the golden rule, so if the reading of the Bible leads to greater compassion and love, the reading is true; if not, it is false.

I think this is a useful and practical way of looking at a text. I am not ultimately making any claim in this book that Elinor Ostrom was on the left, nor even trying with much precision to pigeonhole Ostrom politically. The consensus amongst those who worked with her is that her views were unusual. While it is interesting to look at her views and those of her husband, with whom she worked closely, and their immediate colleagues, my main aim is to make her work accessible and to show how those on the left, especially the ecosocialist left, can make productive use of her diverse and provocative thinking. The intention of Elinor Ostrom's texts was to encourage ways of dealing with practical problems of resource management. If her words inspire action to specifically promote sustainable management of the environment, we have interpreted her words correctly! The extent to which she was radical can be judged by the effects of her work. Measuring effects throws up more problems but I do think it is more useful than a search for some unchanging and intrinsic essence. Thus, this book, chapter by chapter, examines her work and shows how it can be of practical use. In fact, if we do want to pigeonhole her work, I would agree with Paul Dragos Aligică, a former student of the Ostroms', that she might be labelled as a pragmatist (Aligică 2014: 166). A pragmatist in the philosophical sense of thinkers like the American social theorist John Dewey, but most especially in the straightforward sense of trying to solve practical problems. Thus, it has been suggested:

> One of the most interesting aspects of the Ostroms' efforts is the fact that they did not seem to be driven by a doctrinaire philosophy, a rigid code about how social and political science should be done 'correctly' in accordance with some philosophical or epistemological canons. They simply did it, following problems and puzzles they considered interesting or important – to know how things worked or do not work. (Aligică and Sabetti 2014: 4)

While Aligică and other commentators observe that such pragmatism doesn't disguise some core underlying assumptions about both research and politics, problem solving rather than fixed principle was key to her and Vincent's work. Elinor, for example, wasn't specifically concerned with advancing an ideology that was either pro or anti the state, or for or against the market; while her radical democratic ideals are obvious, she started with a question rather than a policy or political demand. The question was how, given the existence of common pool resources, these resources could be conserved. She doggedly addressed this practical problem using the most advanced techniques she could find from social science, ranging from historical case studies to game theory models to experiments.

We can see the ecological crisis as a problem and, as such, take the approach of Ostrom, asking how, precisely, can we deal with such a problem through specific forms of action. One rule that radicals can take from Ostrom is that we should reject slogans and broad principles but instead focus on interventions. We want an ecological society, so rather than simply proclaiming this we need to ask what this means in practice. In dealing with ecological problems she focused most specifically on natural resource commons and in doing so explicitly used perspectives from both social and natural sciences.

MATERIAL EFFECTS

This book aims to encourage greater understanding of Ostrom's work, inspiring others to read her work and act upon it. It does not aim to provide a detailed or exhaustive academic interpretation of her thinking. There are already a number of texts that attempt to do so. These include my own *The Sustainable Economics of Elinor Ostrom* (2014) which provides a PhD-sized academic account of her inspirations and ideas. Other accounts include *Challenging Institutional Analysis and Development: The Bloomington School* (Dragos Aligică and Boettke 2009) and *Elinor Ostrom: An Intellectual Biography* (Tarko 2016). What seems to be missing are popular, accessible accounts of her work that promote engagement with it from commoners, activists and individuals beyond academic corridors.

In attempting to produce a popular account of Elinor's work, I have also been inspired by a number of potential readers. First there are those who have worked closely with her and Vincent Ostrom. I am sure they would wish to see a wider audience for her work but one which does not misrepresent her ideas. I am aware that her ideas are both unusual and easy to wrongly describe. More positively I am also aware that diversity was something she valued and that her ideas were, as noted above, far from stale or fixed. Explaining without over-simplifying is perhaps impossible, or at least difficult, but I feel it is vital to attempt to do so if Ostrom's powerful thoughts are to have a material impact rather than to become a niche intellectual interest.

I am also conscious of students of the Ostroms I have been lucky enough to meet who have been enthused by their work but wanted a left analysis of it. While the Ostroms are difficult to define politically, they definitely did not see themselves as on the conventional left. Nonetheless many on the left have found their work useful and exciting. I have met a fair few people who have studied with the Ostroms, learned from them and been inspired, but wanted to relate what they have learnt to a specifically socialist or left perspective.

I am thinking, most particularly, of readers who have perhaps never heard of Elinor Ostrom or if they have, know only that she shared a prize for her work on commons. Millions of people have been, in recent years, newly inspired by popular movements on the left. In 1989 with the collapse of the Berlin Wall, socialism seemed like a doctrine that would disappear. Not only did the official communism of the Soviet Union disappear but other left alternatives seemed to shrink too. Social Democratic parties like the British Labour Party became dominated by centrist leaders like Tony Blair. In the US the Democrats were Clintonised into a third-way politics of the slick centre. Yet in recent years a new and dynamic left has been dramatically re-emerging. 2015 saw the election of left-wing Labour Party leader Jeremy Corbyn in the UK, and the dramatic bid by the United States' only socialist senator, Bernie Sanders, to challenge Hillary Clinton for the Democrats' Presidential nomination. We have also seen, with the failures of neoliberal finance and increasing economic stagnation, a generalised revolt against conventional economic orthodoxy.

Despite the complexities of Elinor Ostrom's thought, she was unambiguously an advocate of deeper democracy, ecological concern and social equality. I am hoping that this book might attract some of this new dynamic, diverse and populist left to look at her ideas. Alternatives are not self-evident, they need much consideration and careful design. In short, to overcome what we have, alternatives are vital and alternative institutional structures are necessary. Elinor Ostrom's form of institutional economics, given her emphasis on making collective ownership work, is a good start in this regard.

Being against neoliberalism is insufficient to transform neoliberalism, movements and mobilisations have come and gone but have generally failed to sustain major change. Alternatives based on clear institutional analysis can contribute to solutions that move us beyond our current, widely criticised economic system.

BOOK OUTLINE

The title, *Elinor Ostrom's Rules for Radicals*, is inspired, of course, by Saul D. Alinsky, a US rabble rouser, who set out to write a handbook to help those who want to achieve political change. Alinsky was a community organiser who was interested in practical tactics and strategies to win power for communities under threat from powerful interests. He distilled his thoughts into twelve precise pieces of advice. Rule number one, for example, is that 'Power is not only what you have, but what the enemy thinks you have', and rule number twelve suggests, 'Pick the target, freeze it, personalize it, and polarize it' (Alinsky 1971: 130). Elinor Ostrom provides a resource that can help create change and challenge the power of elites. I believe that it is not only Ostrom's commitment to radical demands like equality, deep democracy or ecology that make her important from a left perspective, but more significantly that her work, like Alinsky's, points to a practical politics that can focus our efforts to change society for the better.

Elinor argued that slogans and demands were never enough, we have to take a specific and pragmatic approach to achieve a better society. Alinsky's *Rules for Radicals*, was subtitled *A Pragmatic Primer for Realistic Radicals*: my aim is to use Elinor's work to help resource practical change and to make the apparently impossible achievable.

To this end, the book moves swiftly through her key ideas. Chapter two introduces her most important work on the commons. It presents the reasons why commons are thought to be 'tragic' and thus doomed to fail. After outlining her own path to the commons, the reasons why she thought commons could be made ecologically sustainable are discussed. The design principles she outlined in *Governing the Commons* (1990) are used to explain how tragedy can be overcome and the collective ownership sustained.

Chapter three focuses on environmental problems beyond the commons and green politics. Her contribution to environmental policy making, solutions to climate change and to green politics are described. She wrote in some detail about climate change solutions and, conscious that local solutions were not on their own enough, applied herself to global environmental challenges too. Ostrom can be seen as a political ecologist, concerned with how politics influences our ability to deal with environmental problems. As such her work can contribute to developing a more sophisticated form of green politics. To my knowledge, the links between her analysis and green politics have been largely unexplored. She advocated greater equality, social justice, peace-making and grassroots democracy which, along with ecological sustainability, are core features of green politics.

Chapter four looks at Ostrom's core economics assumptions. Her work on commons allowed her to develop a wider economic analysis. She gently subverted many of the core assumptions of mainstream economics. She was passionate about commons, social sharing and cooperatives, providing practical ideas for building a diverse, ecological and equal economy. While from Occupy to the election of Jeremy Corbyn, demands for a different kind of economy are rising, Ostrom was one of the few thinkers to look at the practicalities of non-state, non-market economics. While she sought to engage with conventional economics rather than sweep it away, her work shows that the foundational assumption that human beings are rational maximisers, locked into selfish and competitive behaviour, can be challenged. Rather than engaging in a broad ideological debate, her approach to economics was based on detailed research and is potentially very useful for those who seek to promote workable alternatives that efficiently provide a more ecological, equal and democratic economy.

Chapter five examines Ostrom's commitment to radical democracy. As noted she believed in deep democracy based on participation rather than top-down structures of authority. Her work on the commons showed her that cooperation for practical conservation is most likely to occur when people have the power to make their own rules, rather than having others tell them what is best to do. Like the green anarchist Murray Bookchin (1986) she was an advocate of direct democracy where possible. Diversity, decentralisation and participation in making popular constitutions were part of her approach to practical politics.

Chapter six shows the relevance of Ostrom's work to feminism and intersectionality. Ostrom can be seen as part of a much wider feminist challenge to economics and is closely linked to feminist economists including Deirdre McCloskey and Marilyn Waring. Many feminist economists suggest that traditional economics, rather than being gender neutral, discriminates against women and has a naive approach to research. Marilyn Waring, a former New Zealand politician wrote *If Women Counted*, in which she argued that measures of economic growth such as Gross National Product ignore the contribution of women (Waring 1989). McCloskey argues that economists claim to be scientific but ignore the influence of culture and metaphor on their work (McCloskey 1985). Ostrom showed that parts of the economy vital to human prosperity and survival, such as commons, are often invisible to economists. Her criticism of conventional economic methodology is also close to those of Waring and McCloskey. For example, like McCloskey, she notes that metaphors, such as the model of the tragedy of the commons, can influence economic policymaking and we should be more conscious of the risks inherent in the construction of misleadingly simplistic narratives.

Ostrom focused on widening participation in politics and economics. This is another area where her ideas will fascinate activists and others concerned with questions of intersectionality. Her anti-essentialist approach to academic work also reflects central debates in twenty-first-century feminism. In a world where resistance to globalisation has given rise to right-wing populist movements that often demonise 'the other' and reject different identities, her embrace of diversity is becoming increasingly relevant. Ostrom is very much a challenge to the politics of Trump, Victor Orban, Erdoğan and Le Pen; political leaders who use race and religion to gain power.

Chapter seven provides a more detailed account of her work on trust and cooperation. The tragedy of the commons was likely to occur if individuals failed to cooperate and the necessary cooperation was only possible if individuals trusted each other. Trust and cooperation are also vital to the creation of an alternative to neoliberalism, as they are essential in creating a more democratic and equal economy. Ostrom used a variety of techniques including experiments to investigate how cooperation and trust could be encouraged. She also felt that global problems such as climate change can be better tackled if practical ways of promoting global cooperation can be promoted. In a world where fear is growing, her approach, which looks pragmatically at building trust, is important. She was, however, aware that there was a negative side to cooperation; for example, firms might cooperate by forming cartels, and in doing so artificially raise prices.

Chapter eight examines her approach to academic research and education. She was fascinated by research methodology because she was aware that different types of methodology could produce different understandings of social reality. The methodology of economists which was based on often simplistic formal models and statistical data led to the notion of the 'tragedy of the commons'. Misleading methodology led to flawed conclusions and, in turn, damaging policies such as the privatisation or nationalisation of the commons. She perceived much academic work as individualist, narrow and elitist. She promoted a radical take on education based on participation. This fed back into her work on ecological economics and democracy. She believed that education should be participatory and that political education should focus on promoting self-organisation. Her ideas were similar to those of the Brazilian radical educationalist Paolo Freire, who believed that the division between teachers and taught should be broken down.

Chapter nine looks at institutional transformation. To achieve change, Ostrom argued, we need to understand institutions. This chapter outlines and critically reviews her Institutional Analysis and Development (IAD) framework to show how it might be used by activists seeking to transform structures. If we understand institutions as based on sets of rules, learning how to map and describe the rules is useful in a variety of ways. For example, Ostrom noted that better institutional design would improve cooperation. Understanding institutions also contributes to changing them and allows less powerful groups in society to challenge exploitation and threats. If we want to challenge neoliberalism we need to understand in detail how neoliberal institutions work. If we wish to create an ecological and democratic economy, we need to evolve appropriate institutions. Ostrom's critical institutionalism is an essential part of her legacy and a source of useful suggestions to radicals who wish to contribute to a more ecological, democratic, diverse and equal future.

Chapter ten concludes by examining both the promise and the limits of her work for practical ecological and social change. Elinor Ostrom was a strong believer in contestation, by which she meant strong critical debate, and it serves her memory and promotes her practice to criticise her ideas so as to develop and adapt them. However, a largely abstract debate is insufficient. She was a practical thinker and we need to ask to what extent her rules for radicals can create practical and positive effects. A Marxist critique is outlined which suggests that she failed to adequately focus on issues of power, structural change and class. An Ostrom critique of Marxism, which suggests that the left often ignores the importance of institutions, is presented. Common features from both Marx and Ostrom are examined, in turn, and criticised. The need for a more sophisticated understanding of cultural politics is suggested. A practical politics, rather than an abstract debate on principles, is an attractive feature of Ostrom's work which is emphasised both in this concluding chapter and throughout this book. This is most obvious in her work on commons which is examined in the next chapter.

2

The Commons:
From Tragedy to Triumph

The term 'common pool resources' is not something that most people have in their everyday language, so let me explain. It's any kind of resource that's bigger than a family backyard pool where it's difficult to keep people out – [because keeping them out is] costly. Anyone who enters may subtract something. So a fishery is pretty obvious. Sometimes it's difficult to figure out who can enter and what the boundaries are, but if I take fish out, that fish isn't available to anyone else. That would be a common pool resource.

(Sullivan 2011)

It appears that Elinor Ostrom's work increasingly focused on commons at least partly as a result of attending a lecture by Garrett Hardin during the 1970s. Hardin, who wrote the 'Tragedy of the Commons' in 1968, was a strong believer in population control, argued that commons showed that human beings could not cooperate to tackle ecological problems. Such a tragedy meant that strong government control was needed to restrain us from damaging our environment. Elinor noted, in a conversation with her friend and fellow political economist Margaret Levi, that Hardin's perspective on population control shocked her:

Hardin gave a speech on the IU [Indiana University, Bloomington] campus, and I went to it, and he indicated the more general – but then it was that he really was worried about population. He indicated that every man and every woman should be sterilized after they have one child. He was very serious about it. [...] I was somewhat taken aback: 'My theory proves that we should do this,' and people said, 'Well, don't you think that that's a little severe?'

'No! That's what we should do, or we're sunk.' Well, he, in my mind, became a totalitarian. (Ostrom 2010d: 8)

Published in the journal *Science* in 1968, the tragedy of the commons suggested that commons would inevitably be destroyed. The solution was to either privatise the commons, selling it off to individual owners who would protect their property, or giving the commons to the government who could prevent its destruction by policing its use. Hardin was not specifically interested in the management of specific commons, instead he saw the commons as an example of a wider problem. He believed that human beings would be unable to make the sacrifices needed to conserve the environment and that environmental problems could only be solved through strong disciplinary measures introduced either in the form of economic incentives or state action.

Hardin argued that environmental problems are largely a product of population growth. More people consuming more resources would wreck the biosphere, so zero population growth or even a cut in human numbers was essential. Hardin suggested our approach to child bearing can be related to the problem of a commons. Essentially, we might believe that we have to reduce the population to conserve the environment but we are also aware that if we have fewer children, others will continue to reproduce and so our individual effort will have a negligible effect on the overall population level. Thus, if we make a sacrifice, others will not. They will exploit our good action and, in the parlance of some, play us for suckers. This is an illustration of what economists term a free rider problem. If one person pays or makes a sacrifice and others do not, this erodes the willingness of those who would contribute to do so. In the end, nobody makes a sacrifice and disaster ensues. This is perhaps an odd way of looking at child bearing, given the challenges of giving birth and childcare, but odd or not, this was Hardin's core concern.

Hardin used the analogy of common land to illustrate his thesis. Specifically, he used the term 'tragic' in the sense of a Greek or Shakespearian tragedy, not only was the outcome grim but it was also inevitable despite the good intentions and constructive desires of the individuals involved.

The tragedy of the commons develops in this way. Picture a pasture open to all. It is to be expected that each herdsman will try to keep as many cattle as possible on the commons. Such an arrangement may work reasonably satisfactorily for centuries because tribal wars, poaching, and disease keep the numbers of both man and beast well below the carrying capacity of the land. Finally, however, comes the day of reckoning, that is, the day when the long-desired goal of social stability becomes a reality. At this point, the inherent logic of the commons remorselessly generates tragedy.

As a rational being, each herdsman seeks to maximize his gain. Explicitly or implicitly, more or less consciously, he asks, 'What is the utility *to me* of adding one more animal to my herd?' This utility has one negative and one positive component.

1) The positive component is a function of the increment of one animal. Since the herdsman receives all the proceeds from the sale of the additional animal, the positive utility is nearly +1.

2) The negative component is a function of the additional overgrazing created by one more animal. Since, however, the effects of overgrazing are shared by all the herdsmen, the negative utility for any particular decision-making herdsman is only a fraction of –1.

Adding together the component partial utilities, the rational herdsman concludes that the only sensible course for him to pursue is to add another animal to his herd. And another; and another . . . But this is the conclusion reached by each and every rational herdsman sharing a commons. Therein is the tragedy. Each man is locked into a system that compels him to increase his herd without limit – in a world that is limited. Ruin is the destination toward which all men rush, each pursuing his own best interest in a society that believes in the freedom of the commons. Freedom in a commons brings ruin to all. (Hardin 1968: 1243–1244).

Writing in the late 1960s Hardin reflected a growing neo-Malthusian environmental concern. Thomas Malthus (1766–1834) was an early classical economist along with Adam Smith and David Ricardo. He argued that human numbers tend to grow faster than agricultural yields. Thus poverty, rather than being a function of social class inequality, was a fact of human nature. If we had more food, more children would survive into adulthood, leading back to poverty and starvation. Attempts to promote social justice and end poverty were thus futile. Hardin and other neo-Malthusians applied this analysis to environmental problems and Hardin specifically used the notion of 'The Tragedy of the Commons' as a justification for their need for harsh population control.

He argues that because individuals cannot cooperate to deal with the alleged threat of over population, we need to sacrifice our liberty to a strong state that will police our actions. He notes, of course, that actual commons can be privatised or run by the state, but his real concern is in advocating strong central authority to limit population and to restrict our ability to damage the environment.

His rather bleak view of ecological management is reflected in another of his essays, 'Lifeboat Ethics: The Case Against Helping the Poor'. He suggests that the environment can be compared to a life boat. If we are on a life boat, having escaped from a sinking ship and we allow too many other survivors on to the boat, it will sink. Our compassion fails to help others and we drown too. Compassion, for Hardin, is a vice rather than a virtue:

> So here we sit, say 50 people in our lifeboat. To be generous, let us assume it has room for 10 more, making a total capacity of 60. Suppose the 50 of us in the lifeboat see 100 others swimming in the water outside, begging for admission to our boat or for handouts. We have several options: we may be tempted to try to live by the Christian ideal of being 'our brother's keeper,' or by the Marxist ideal of 'to each according to his needs.' Since the needs of all in the water are the same, and since they can all be seen as 'our brothers,' we could take them all into our boat, making a total of 150 in a boat designed for 60. The boat swamps, everyone drowns. Complete justice, complete catastrophe. (Hardin 1977: 263)

Hardin further noted that global environment can be seen as a commons and if we don't create strong central control, catastrophe will result. For Hardin 'spaceship ethics' based on sharing and solidarity with those in need was wrong. Morality was immoral because good intentions, according to his analysis, led to tragedy for all. 'The fundamental error of spaceship ethics, and the sharing it requires, is that it leads to what I call "the tragedy of the commons." Under a system of private property, the men who own property recognize their responsibility to care for it, for if they don't they will eventually suffer' (Hardin 1977: 264).

Hardin advocated that children should be taught the 'tragedy' and argued that sharing and help for others whether justified by Christianity or socialism, should be strongly opposed. 'One of the major tasks of education today should be the creation of such an acute awareness of the dangers of the commons that people will recognize its many varieties. For example, the air and water have become polluted because they are treated as commons' (Hardin 1977: 265).

Hardin argued that his views are backed up by a long historical tradition that can be can be traced back to Aristotle. Indeed, the Ancient Greek philosopher claimed:

> What is common to the greatest number gets the least amount of care. Men pay most attention to what is their own; they care less for what is common; or at any rate they care for it only to the extent to which each is individually concerned. Even when there is no other cause for inattention, men are more prone to neglect their duty when they think that another is attending to it. (Aristotle 1946: 1261b)

The mathematician William Forster Lloyd published an anti-commons tract in 1833 which made use of similar arguments. He asked 'Why are the cattle on a common so puny and stunted? Why is the common itself so bare-worn, and cropped so differently from the adjoining inclosures?' (Lloyd 1833: 30). His answer was that collective care for the commons led to poor livestock management and generalised misery.

While Hardin's notions of the tragedy of the commons and the life boat thesis seem unpalatable, they are merely the narrative gloss on a logical argument that suggests that without strong coercive action, environmental destruction is inevitable. This logic has a history and apparently evidence to back it up, so why did Elinor Ostrom feel that commons might conserve resources and produce sleek and healthy rather than thin and puny cattle?

CONSERVING THE COMMONS

Elinor Ostrom put huge intellectual effort into investigating how the commons could be made to work. She didn't believe that the commons was perfect or automatically a better option than private property or state ownership. She didn't oppose private ownership nor was she an anarchist libertarian who rejected all government intervention. She had, however, seen working commons, and the contrast with an academic literature that said this was impossible, or at least unlikely, inspired her. Her starting point was to look at examples of common pool resources which were managed successfully as common pool property.

In studying this question, she was careful to distinguish between common pool resources and common pool property. Common pool resources include forests, pasture land and fisheries where it is difficult to exclude users, thus they tend to be open to collective use. Common pool property is a legal category that provides for collective ownership. A thing is not the same as the legal form of ownership it takes. She also noted that legal notions of ownership were more diverse than is often assumed. Thus, common pool property may not be the same as a common pool resource.

She examined long-term historical case studies of successfully managed commons, i.e. common pool resources that were collectively owned. These were contrasted with examples of commons that had failed. Detailed examination of both failed and successful commons allowed her to develop some ideas as to how the potential 'tragedy of the commons' might be overcome. Incidentally, despite her obvious negative reaction to hearing Hardin speak at Bloomington, she did see the 'tragedy of the commons' as a problem that demanded investigation, and grappled with it rather than dismissing it. She went so far as to open a correspondence with Hardin, engaging him in debate and inviting him around for dinner. According to Barbara Allen, who was one of the Ostroms' students who attended, 'the conversation was vigorous' and Elinor made hamburgers (Harford 2013).

She was also aware that in order to study commons it was important to aggregate research, so as to find a way of collecting data from different sources. This was difficult because commons had been studied by a very wide variety of academics from different disciplines. She and Vincent were political economists and had a good insight into research from other economists and political scientists, however ecologists, hydrologists, anthropologists, geographers, legal theorists and many others had looked at the commons too. She set out to create a common language for studying the commons; as we shall see, language and culture were important to her in understanding human society and ecological problems. It is already clear how ambitious and unusual her approach was. She took formal models that were rooted in economics, looked at historical evidence which suggested that models might be limited and during her career added new layers of analysis including ecology and psychology to her enduring core interest in political institutions. As we shall see in later chapters, Ostrom's approach to academic research is both radical and instructive. She was certainly a busy woman, no simple solutions for her. Complexity and multiple research methods kept her occupied for decades.

Governing the Commons, which was published in 1990, summarised much of her work in the 1970s and 1980s. At the core of the book are studies of what she termed long-enduring, self-organised and self-governed common pool resource systems, which are contrasted with examples of failed commons. She looked at the communal ownership of high mountain meadows in Törbel, Switzerland, along with three Japanese village commons and community irrigation systems in Spain and the Philippines. These were all based on secondary documentary work rather than her own first-hand experience. All had existed as communal managed resource systems for hundreds of years and provided documentation as to how such management had occurred.

The anthropologist Robert Netting discussed Törbel in his book *Balancing on an Alp* (1981). Villagers owned private plots to grow vegetables but the mixed landscape and need for summer and winter pastures made private ownership of all land inconvenient. Much of the pasture land was owned as commons; the local villagers had made up their own rules for management to prevent over grazing. Netting discovered that legal documents could be found from as far back as 1224. The Japanese commons were studied by a political scientist, Margaret McKean, who provides an account of long use and successful management (McKean 1982). In contrast to Hardin's bleak assumptions McKean noted that in studying the Japanese examples she had 'not yet turned up an example of a commons that suffered ecological destruction while it was still a commons' (cited in Ostrom 1990: 65). The irrigation examples from Spain and the Philippines also used historical records to indicate how institutional rules had been put in place to maintain collective systems of ownership and use. Elinor also supplemented these studies with her work and that of Vincent and their colleagues on collective water basin management in California. Failed commons included the fragile Nova Scotia inshore fisheries, a flawed irrigation project in Sri Lanka, Turkish fisheries with continuing commons management problems and examples of unsuccessful ground water basin management.

Having put all these case studies together and examined them with care, Elinor was at first mystified. There seemed to be nothing in common between the different commons that worked. To take the example of Törbel, Netting noted that it was atypical and that there were many different sorts of commons management in the Swiss Alps. Törbel worked as a form of collective management but so did other Swiss commons with different structures. Ostrom was an advocate of diversity but the diversity of forms of commons management seemed to her to be overwhelming. Continued study suggested to her that there was no blueprint for a successful system of commons management. Ultimately, however, she came up with eight design rules which were based on similarities she found from looking at the various long-lasting commons.

First, sustainable commons, she believed, needed to have clearly defined boundaries. This meant that while they might be used communally there was not a free-for-all; commoners in a defined community had access but this was not open to all passers-by. Enclosure is normally thought to mean that a commons is fenced off and taken away from the commoners, yet according to Elinor Ostrom some kind of fencing process is needed to conserve the commons for the community who use it.

If there was a defined community who used the commons, they would have a long-term interest in conserving the commons. If others came in and took from the commons, they could move on and had no interest in long-term conservation. So, keeping some kind of secure boundary for the commons made it easier to reduce the problem of free riders.

Secondly, the rules for commons use had to fit local circumstances, so they would work effectively. What worked in one locality might be inappropriate in another. Different commons would have different environmental conditions, so would have to be treated in different ways. The common land known as 'North Meadow' near the English village of Cricklade would be opened up for animals to graze on Lammas Day, 12 August. This is the date chosen because by then the hay would have been harvested. While the hay was growing, individuals used particular parcels of land that were rented but on Lammas Day the Meadow reverted to common grazing. August 12th is a date that works for a system that shifted from cereal cultivation to grazing in southern England but would be inappropriate in other parts of the world for other agricultural systems. Ostrom felt that some kind of committee establishing precise commons rules over a whole country or region would fail. This doesn't mean that all decisions must be local and she was aware that regional, national and international decision making was needed, in some circumstances, but it was clear to her that local ecology is diverse and locally established rules were a better starting point than standard prescriptions.

A third design feature is that the individuals who use a commons need to be able to participate in the making and modifying of rules. Individuals are more likely to respect rules that they have helped construct. Self-governance is thus likely to be more effective, compared to governance by others. It is important to ration access to common resource to avoid overuse and subsequent potential degradation. Such rationing will involve sacrifice, but sacrifice which has been negotiated by members of the community is more likely to be agreed to than a sacrifice determined by an external body. This contradicts Hardin's belief that top-down control is more effective than governance by commoners.

A fourth feature is effective monitoring. Boundaries and effective rules will only work if they are policed in some way. Norms of good behaviour, while useful, are unlikely to be sufficient in protecting a commons on their own. The first step to effective policing is via effective monitoring. An individual or individuals need to record any infractions of the rules. Thus, in the Japanese examples discussed by McKean, a constable may be hired. The West Basin water users employed a water master. Monitoring is a way of making sure that the free rider problem is overcome by identifying those who ignore the rules and exploit a resource.

In medieval Europe a number of different officials were put in place to observe the use of the commons. Posts created in Anglo-Saxon England are still used to monitor commons in the UK in the twenty-first century. 'A manorial or community officer involved in the managing and policing of agrarian resources and common land.' Terms and duties varied between manors. For example, a 'common reeve' was usually appointed to manage and police stock on the common; a 'moss reeve' would police the cutting of peat for fuel. Some manor courts appointed a number of resource-specific officers known as 'lookers': e.g. a hedge looker to check that boundaries were maintained, and a peat looker to regulate peat cutting.

A fifth feature was the use of graduated sanctions. A sanction is a punishment of some kind for breaking the rules established to conserve a commons. Clearly, some kind of punishment or sanction is necessary as it is unlikely that good will will on its own will prevent abuse of the commons. Free riders need to be sanctioned or else they will abuse the commons and depletion may occur. However, Ostrom's research suggested that sanctions should be carefully graded from soft to more severe. In many cases users might break a rule without being conscious of doing so, a simple warning will remind them of the rules. To use strong punishment for a first offence might be costly and cause resentment which could make the system more difficult to sustain. The Japanese example where commoners might be fined in sake which was then used to pay the constables who policed the commons is a good example. Informal and gentle sanctions are likely at first. A fisher who broke commons rules, perhaps going out to sea on fallow days when fishing was banned, might wait a long time before being served in a local public house. The idea of a 'grim trigger', a term used by game theorists to refer to an automatic rule of excluding someone from the game if they did not cooperate, was found to be counterproductive by Ostrom.

A sixth feature is low-cost conflict resolution. Elinor Ostrom noted that rules, even if simple and agreed by participants, can be interpreted in different ways. Such differences can be mediated by an agreed judicial body even if it is highly informal. She also suggested that such mechanisms could make it more difficult for a local elite to take control of the resource. The substitution of local manorial courts, which managed the English commons, by more distant and formal bodies may have been one factor that led to the decline of the commons.

English commons formed in the Anglo-Saxon period relied on some form of local body to manage conflicts and if necessary to punish those who broke the commons rules. The Court Leet, for example, still meets in Cricklade, Wiltshire and is responsible for grazing on North Meadow. Interestingly, the courts were originally a system of popular democracy with much wider powers. Every ten individuals would elect a representative to sit on the court and make decisions about local politics and government.

Elinor Ostrom also felt that her research suggested that 'minimal recognition of rights to organise' was a seventh essential requirement for a successful commons. Recognition of the rights of the commoners to maintain their own commons was vital to conservation. Control from above may disrupt the maintenance of a commons system. More fundamentally, many commons have been privatised or taken into state control. Paternalistic regulation from external authorities can also be damaging because while it may be well meaning, it is often insensitive to local conditions. External regulation also reduces the possibility of self-governance which is necessary, according to Ostrom, for a commons to work well. Commons have often been taken over by external authorities and destroyed. This is the history of the indigenous commons that dominated the USA and continues to be repeated. The political factors eroding commons are important to understand and can nullify well designed and maintained local systems of governance.

Finally, she argued, as an eighth point, that commons need to be part of nested enterprises, i.e. they work within wider systems. So, a commons might be part of a river estuary, which might be part of a larger region, and so on. Environments are not discrete islands, and even islands are influenced by weather systems and oceans. Despite Ostrom's emphasis on boundaries, common property systems may overlap with inter-communing occurring between different communities. There must, therefore, be ways of negotiating the links between inter locking commons. Irrigation is one good example of this principle. A local irrigation system which is run as a commons may well be part of a wider water network. Unless local commons can work with other systems, failure will be likely.

There are many instances of commons facing degradation that have been rescued by commoners, using the design points noted by Ostrom, to conserve them. A good example is Boston Common in the United States.

> [T]he town agreed that no individual could keep more than one cow on the Common, or four sheep in place of a cow. It enforced the rules by appointing a town keeper, who received a fee for every cow and sheep and lamb. People often tested the limits, but the system worked through eight generations. It succeeded because the town combined the idea of the common with the institution of the town meeting [. . .] In the end there was nothing of the 'tragedy of the commons' on Boston Common. (Fischer 2000: 128)

Boston Common was established in 1634 and while no longer used for grazing remains a public shared amenity. In English commons systems 'stints' were organised to prevent over grazing or other forms of exploitation. A good example is the rule that a commoner cannot place more animals on a commons than the commoner can feed over the winter when the cattle or sheep would be removed from the commons. The very simple idea of a stint seemed to have been forgotten by Hardin. While in theory such forms of rationing might be difficult to maintain, in practice, they often worked well. The use of stints continues for common land in England and Wales in the twenty-first century:

A 'stint' or 'gait' is a pasture right defined as a fixed number of animals. Thus a common or pasture may be said to be 'stinted': each grazier holds a certain number of stints, and a formula adjusts their value for different livestock (e.g. one stint = one ewe with lamb, four stints = one horse, etc.). The stinting formulae vary between commons and pastures. A stint is sometimes expressed in terms of a 'beastgate' or 'cattlegate' (the right to graze one horned beast on common land), with a formula which converts the beastgate into alternative types of livestock (e.g. one beastgate = ten sheep. (Institutions for Collective Action, Glossary – Commons – England and Wales)

Elinor Ostrom also used experimental methods and game theory to refine her understanding of how cooperation to conserve the commons could be best maintained. Her examination of this is discussed in greater detail in chapter seven. She combined historical data with formal modelling, statistics with qualitative work; drawing widely on a battery of research techniques, she even used satellite surveys and investigated the role of linguistics. Her work was endless and energetic because she knew that the commons was an important area of study with big implications for economics, ecological management and much else.

Ostrom, while showing that privatisation or government control might fail, did not advocate the commons as a universal solution. Commons fitted with her commitment to deep democracy and community based solutions but she strongly rejected one size fits all solutions. She was also worried that commons might be imposed from above, noting a destructive fashion for central governments to suddenly relinquish control of resources that local communities were not equipped to deal with:

But the resources have been taken away, degraded and then given back in a one- or two-hour meeting. I have been to some of those meetings and it is rather incredible. They bring the local people into a hall. They say 'now you own x'; they give them a little bit of background of what they must do now; tell the people that they are responsible; and then walk away. (Ostrom et al. 2012: 81–82)

Commons need care and communing to make them work. Collective ownership can work well but it takes time; simply proclaiming a commons or giving back land to a local community without careful preparation may lead to disaster. Ostrom found that the tragedy of the commons can be overcome, but this involved thought and care to craft rules and institutions that sustain commons. Ostrom argued that ecological problems are political, so can be tackled by thoughtful governance. However, despite her success in studying the commons and moving us from a fear of tragedy to a potential delight in the power of the commons, she has been criticised for being too much of a localist thinker (Harvey 2012). Yet while she felt that local management was often essential, she also analysed wider and less local environmental problems such as global climate change. Chapter three examines her contribution to environmental management on a wider scale and the links between her work and green politics.

3

Climate Change, Ecology and Green Politics

We have a decade to act before the economic cost of current viable solutions becomes too high. Without action, we risk catastrophic and perhaps irreversible changes to our life-support system. Our primary goal must be to take planetary responsibility for this risk, rather than placing in jeopardy the welfare of future generations.

(Ostrom 2012)

In an article entitled 'Green from the grassroots', published in June 2012, the very month when Elinor Ostrom died of cancer, she put out a passionate call for action on global ecological problems. Often seen as concentrating on local environmental management, she became increasingly concerned with international problems such as climate change. This chapter introduces her concept of social-ecological systems that she used to see how individual commons fitted into wider networks. Her perspectives on international environmental problems such as climate change and ocean conservation are examined. In turn, her contribution to the construction of a radical and effective green politics is discussed. While not a member of a green party her core concerns with ecological sustainability, greater equality, peace-making, deep democracy and diversity are shared with most green parties.

SOCIAL-ECOLOGICAL SYSTEMS

Elinor Ostrom and indeed Vincent Ostrom were interested in resource management and fascinated by the challenge the tragedy of the commons and similar models pose for cooperation to manage the commons. This meant, as we have seen, that much of her research was based upon a detailed study of local commons management. Despite this localism Elinor Ostrom was aware that any commons was likely to be part of a wider system. Even if local people can cooperate to conserve the commons, external threats can make sustainable management difficult. North Meadow in Cricklade, Wiltshire, has been cited already as a historic commons that is maintained in the twenty-first century. It follows the design features such as a clear boundary, monitoring and low-cost conflict resolution identified in *Governing the Commons* and has worked well for over a thousand years, providing agricultural land while maintaining rich wildlife. The meadow floods in winter, the rich deposits of Thames river mud fertilise it. Yet because of climate change extreme weather conditions potentially threaten it. In 2016, exceptional rain made the meadow flood right into April; the meadow was closed to walkers and there were fears that it would be disrupted. In 2013 the fritillaries had failed to flower at all because of continual flooding:

> North Meadow is situated between two rivers, the Thames and the Churn, and is seasonally flooded every year; but in the summer of 2012, the wettest on record in England, it never became unflooded. It was under water the whole time and, indeed, is only drying out now. This meant that the hay in this hay meadow could not be harvested last July and August; it could not be taken off, and it remains there, a thickly packed, flat mat over all the ground, through which virtually nothing – certainly not the fragile fritillary stems – can penetrate. There has been a colossal smothering, truly weird to witness. (McCarthy 2013)

Ostrom was correct to note that successful commons are nested into wider systems. She increasingly theorised ecological management in terms not just of discrete commons but wider social-ecological systems. Cricklade's North Meadow can be seen as part of a wider social-ecological system that includes the upper reaches of the river Thames. In turn, this social-ecological system is shaped by climate change which is a global phenomenon.

Specifically, Ostrom sought to understand how social-ecological systems (SESs) worked, so they can be maintained in a sustainable way. This, of course, was a challenging undertaking that was still incomplete when she died. She did come to a number of provisional conclusions which give us some inspiration in constructing more sophisticated forms of environmental management. A good summary of her work can be found in the 2009 paper 'A General Framework for Analyzing Sustainability of Social-Ecological Systems'. In this paper, she observed,

> the world is currently threatened by considerable damage to or losses of many natural resources, including fisheries, lakes, and forests, as well as experiencing major reductions in biodiversity and the threat of massive climatic change. All humanly used resources are embedded in complex, social-ecological systems (SESs). SESs are composed of multiple subsystems and internal variables within these subsystems at multiple levels analogous to organisms composed of organs, organs of tissues, tissues of cells, cells of proteins, etc. (Ostrom 2009a: 419)

Commons could be seen as parts of larger SESs and this insight reflects Elinor's eighth design rule for a successful commons that it needs to be nested into a large system or sub-systems that are also sustainably managed.

A social-ecological system is inevitably complex. To deal with any form of environmental management there is a social dimension which needs to take account of human institutions and behaviour. This throws up vast debates about politics, economics and sociology. Ostrom was adamant that ecological policies were far from obvious because what works in terms of politics and other disciplines of human society is the subject of intense debate. Too often, environmental protection is presented as desirable but the need for socially sophisticated policy is a distant afterthought. Human beings are embedded within the rest of nature and any management of SESs requires a strong understanding of ecology and other natural sciences. Elinor argued that we should embrace complexity and keep refining our understanding of both social and natural sciences, noting 'we must learn how to dissect and harness complexity, rather than eliminate it from such systems'. (Ostrom 2009: 420)

She was very keen, as with her work on the commons, to construct a common language with shared terminology that would allow improved communication between academics, noting the 'process is complicated, however, because entirely different frameworks, theories, and models are used by different disciplines to analyse their parts of the complex multilevel whole'. It is also worth noting that while she believed academic work was vital, she felt that the communities who lived and worked within SESs would often understand them far better than academics. As will be discussed later, Ostrom's approach to academic work was deeply democratic and she was sceptical of the idea that academics always had expertise and non-academics were always ignorant. Nonetheless creating common terminology was seen as a way of making it easier to understand environmental problems so that they could better be solved.

Ostrom was interested in using a framework to understand such systems. Her framework was like an alphabet, an intellectual tool case, that could be used to describe a particular situation. Her frameworks have been criticised as being over complex, however, not all of the potential factors need to be included. A list of ecological and social influences can be very long indeed but not all are used for a particular SES because not all are relevant. A good SES framework is like a map which helps us understand a real-life situation. If the map is too detailed it will be too big to use, if it isn't detailed enough it will not be much use to navigate by. The general SES framework evolved from her Institutional Analysis and Development (IAD) framework which is described in chapter nine.

A good example of the use of an SES framework is the study of a cooperative project for harvesting turtle eggs in Ostional on the Pacific coast of Costa Rica. The community is unique in being able to harvest eggs from the olive ridley turtle (*Lepidochelys olivacea*) legally. The study was used to assess how this practice could be environmentally sustainable and economically beneficial to the community. While the turtles could be studied as a species within a commons, the commons being a 14 kilometre stretch of beach, they were embedded within a wider system. So, the sustainable harvest depended not just on the Ostional community but was influenced by political and ecological factors that affected the turtles as they moved through the

Pacific Ocean. Thus, researchers noted that 'the system boundaries (RS2) seem to be particularly clear in the sense that turtles, like frogs and toads, always return to their place of birth to lay eggs – in our case a beach approximately fourteen kilometers long', but was part of a larger system (Schlüter and Madrigal 2012: 158).

The project perhaps surprisingly benefitted both local people and turtle conservation. Ten thousand eggs are produced by the initial wave of turtles. Without collection, most would simply rot and it would be difficult for eggs to hatch safely. A biologist helps set quotas, and monitoring and sanctioning consistent with Elinor's commons design rules are used successfully. The SES framework was used to assess wider challenges to this sustainable community conservation effort. For example, the gender of turtles is affected by the temperature of the sand and climate change is likely to influence this.

The conclusion that this project promotes conservation is challenged by some who argue that any harvesting of eggs can be termed poaching, and makes it difficult to restrict more damaging harvesting. A blanket ban on any harvesting of eggs might be more effective at maintaining turtle populations. Ostrom's approach broadly rejects blanket bans on exploitation if ecological management is possible but blanket bans might be easier to enforce. In turn, by making all exploitation illegal this may criminalise communities who have an interest in long-term conservation. Ostional villagers who lived by the sea shore were criminalised and subject to eviction before a more sensitive system of conservation was introduced. An SES approach does not, intrinsically, point to one conservation policy but it shows that complexity and unintended consequences need to be addressed. Environmental sustainability is difficult, and demanding; it is insufficient to provide practices and policies without careful elaboration, development and testing. Conservation policies must be adapted to particular contexts and potential consequences must be assessed. From Elinor Ostrom's perspective, one size never fits all.

SEAS, OCEANS AND FISHERIES

Elinor Ostrom was particularly concerned with seas, oceans and fisheries. When asked about the most important environment challenge beyond climate change by the German magazine *Spiegel*, she replied

> The oceans! They are being threatened to an ever greater degree. It is a disaster, a very difficult situation. The fish resources are over-exploited and waste, including CO_2, is dumped in huge quantities into the ocean. The law of the sea has not been effective at all. A lot of fishing ships act like roving bandits. That's why better ocean governance is one of the top priorities for safeguarding the future. (Spiegel online 2009)

She was conscious of what the institutional economist Mancur Olson has termed 'roving bandit' economies, where individuals or firms might enter an environment, take resources and then move on. Unlike communities seeking to live from fisheries or other resources for many generations the 'bandits' were only interested in short-term profit and could wreck an environment through over fishing or other forms of over exploitation. This incidentally is about as close Ostrom ever got to criticising capitalism; she and Vincent argued that market economies could be embedded in ecologically sustainable systems.

Ostrom felt that the threat of such 'roving bandits' might demand government intervention to protect individual fishing communities and the fish from being made extinct. However, if protection policies were inflexible they might also do harm. Certainly, Elinor Ostrom was critical of the European Union's Common Fisheries Policy noting, 'Well, it is rather tragic because the European fisheries rules go all the way from the Mediterranean to the Baltic. And it's one set of rules for all that. The Baltic is an entirely different ecological system and it just doesn't make sense' (Ostrom et al. 2012: 37). So while international agreements on fisheries are vital, Ostrom argued that they might need to be implemented in different ways in different places. She also felt that local communities had an interest in avoiding over fishing so they could sustain their livelihoods into the future, and might have much expertise in doing so.

CLIMATE CHANGE

Climate change became a focal concern. Elinor Ostrom was a strong critic of those who denied that climate change was occurring because of human action and signed a letter in defence of scientists who were being silenced by climate deniers. Her work on game theory has an obvious application to global climate talks. The prisoner's dilemma applies to countries bargaining over how much to reduce emissions by. The prisoner's dilemma assumes that there are two prisoners, both arrested by the police, who are held in separate cells and cannot communicate with each other. The police do not have quite enough evidence to charge them. If both prisoners refuse to confess they will be set free. Yet it is assumed in the model that both prisoners will tend to confess because they fear betrayal by each other. The authorities say to each prisoner that they will receive a reduced sentence if they are the first to confess. If both kept quiet both would go free for lack of evidence, however if one confesses both go to prison, so fearing that the other will confess and gain a shorter sentence both will confess.

The prisoner's dilemma has been used to argue that human cooperation including cooperation to protect the environment is unlikely. Ostrom spent much of her career thinking about the prisoner's dilemma and how cooperation could be nurtured. A later chapter will look in more detail at her attempts to model human cooperation and to overcome dilemmas that require some sacrifice. However, while she supported global climate agreements, she did not think they were enough. In several papers and articles she promoted a 'polycentric' approach to climate change. Polycentricism was an important concept for her and Vincent; instead of thinking that organisations worked best when they had one leader and a strong chain of command, the Ostroms felt that diversity made for better decision making. This was because the idea of a godlike leader or committee with perfect information is a myth. Learning tends to be collective and overlapping authorities reduce the chance of mistakes being made. Polycentricism promotes good decision making and is appropriate given the complexity and uncertainty of many social and ecological problems.

The polycentric approach to climate change meant tackling the problem at multiple possible levels from the individual to the local community, through regions and on to countries as well as on a global scale. Elinor also felt that waiting for a global agreement to occur wasted time; while efforts were made at a global level, we could still without such agreement tackle climate change at other levels. For example, while she was dismayed that the US government under George Bush Jr was at a federal level ignoring climate change, she was pleased that many major US cities were taking action independently.

Unsurprisingly, as a cautious advocate of complexity, she felt some of the methods being used to challenge climate change were simplistic and likely to fail. While she argued that market mechanisms had their role in an economy, she felt that carbon trading and carbon pricing were not always effective solutions to climate change. She also emphasised that indigenous peoples who protected forests that acted as a carbon sink should be supported. She did not think that individual action was sufficient but clearly saw lifestyle change to reduce carbon emissions as part of the picture. When I met her in 2012, shortly before her untimely death, she was enthusiastic about the solar panels she had fitted to her home. Again, while she often thought government action might be inappropriate she was pleased to see subsidies to make it cheaper for citizens to install solar power and other forms of renewable energy.

She also argued that an effective way of promoting action to slow or prevent climate change was to point out additional benefits that might be made from tackling it. If reducing energy use or switching to renewable makes our lives better, we are more likely to take such action. Ostrom felt that cutting carbon could promote healthier living and a better environment to live in.

In her interview with *Spiegel* she praised the effort of the city of Freiburg, which she saw as a good example of such a positive approach to climate change action:

I spend quite a bit of time in Germany and I'm very impressed by some of the local action I see. Local action cannot do it fully, but just think about all the bicycle-paths that they have built there. That is a case where the action of individuals is reducing emissions. At the same time it is a very healthy thing. On Sundays everybody is going to the woods and has a good time on their bikes – and not in their cars. It's good for your health and for the environment. So everyone should ask himself: Why don't I bike to work and leave the damn car at home or get rid of it entirely? (Spiegel online 2009)

She tended, surprisingly perhaps for a political economist, to be a rather frugal character. She and Vincent built much of their own furniture and helped build their home and holiday retreat. She often remarked that she was born poor, noting the privations of the 1930s and 40s with perhaps some pride. However, she was clear that advocating a hair-shirt existence was not an effective way of increasing support for environmental policies. Her work on commons noted implicitly the material economic benefits of successful commons management. In discussing climate change she argued that reducing use of CO_2 by burning less coal, gas and oil had other clear benefits. Reducing pollution from burning fossil fuels improves air quality. She also noted that reducing dependency on cars and promoting cycling brought benefits in terms of health and general wellbeing.

Her approach shows both a sympathy with and an advance on two broad approaches to climate change. She was unconvinced by sceptics who denied the problem but maintained a critical attitude to much climate policy, climate policy had to be judged with unintended consequences and complex systems in mind. So she might be seen as a climate sceptic in this specific sense. She was also sympathetic, as noted, to an approach of living lightly on the Earth, using fewer resources and using them with care, but well aware that for policies to gain support they had to improve peoples' lives. Not many thinkers combine support for using fewer resources with a caution about the potential pitfalls and unintended consequences of environmental policy making.

GREEN POLITICS

Elinor Ostrom's politics were complex and she never engaged in party political work, however she shared a number of concerns with members of the green movement and green parties. She was a keen advocate of equality, diversity, grassroots democracy, peaceful solutions, cooperation and, of course, environmental protection, all Green Party principles.

She advocated the seven-generation rule, noting that long-term sustainability was essential, so that when we make decisions we should think of generations unborn far into the future.

Our problem is how to craft rules at multiple levels that enable humans to adapt, learn, and change over time so that we are sustaining the very valuable natural resources that we inherited so that we may be able to pass them on. I am deeply indebted to the indigenous peoples in the U.S. who had an image of seven generations being the appropriate time to think about the future. I think we should all reinstate in our mind the seven-generation rule. When we make really major decisions, we should ask not only what will it do for me today, but what will it do for my children, my children's children, and their children's children into the future. (Ostrom 2008)

Seven Generations

She and Vincent were literal political ecologists long before people had heard of green parties, focusing on how political processes shaped our interactions with the environment.

The emphasis on principles or fixed policy demands tended to be implicit, understated and in the background for Elinor Ostrom. This is the opposite of much Green Party and radical environmental politics, indeed it is distinct from most politics. A set of essential values are outlined, these are translated into particular policies and then the aim is to sell them to the electorate so as win power and implement them. For example, the German Greens in their 1983 manifesto for the then West German Bundestag, put forward four key elements of a green platform: ecology, social justice, non-violence and grassroots democracy (Die Gruenen 1983). Each green party then has specific policies that reflect these and other fundamental values such as the Green Party of England and Wales' opposition to fracking. While political parties need policies and protest movements make demands, this was not the central concern of Elinor Ostrom.

Ostrom viewed ecological problems as profoundly political. Human beings are part of nature, hence part of ecology, and the politics of humanity has an influence on the rest of nature. Her kind of political ecology contrasts both with much mainstream politics and much green politics. Political ideologies have on the whole tended to ignore ecological problems and challenges. Occasionally political thinkers in history have examined environmental challenges, for example, Friedrich Engels wrote about ecology and John Stuart Mill discussed the negative effects of growth on our surroundings. Peter Kropotkin and William Morris are examples of other ecological thinkers who were important contributors to wider political traditions. Nonetheless environmental questions have generally been ignored by most anarchists, socialists, conservatives and liberals.

While there are deep roots to green politics, green parties first began to be founded in the early 1970s. Many prominent environmental pressure groups like Greenpeace and Friends of the Earth also came into existence at approximately the same time. During the late 1960s and early 1970s there was a wave of concern around global environmental problems such as generalised pollution and the problems associated with nuclear power. The Green Party of England and Wales was originally founded as PEOPLE in 1973 before being renamed the Ecology Party in 1975. Much of this concern was Malthusian and Garrett Hardin's 'Tragedy of the Commons' was an early influence. While Hardin's view was more conservative and pessimistic, reports like *The Limits to Growth* and *Blueprint for Survival* argued in similar vein that over population and continued economic growth threatened humanity and the rest of nature. As already noted, Ostrom's view was that 'tragedy' might be averted without drastic measures to restrict human freedom.

An alternative to this rather Malthusian political ecology can be seen in the cornucopian vision of thinkers like Julian Simon, a Maryland-based professor of business and economics. Cornucopian refers to the classical Greek notion of a horn of plenty. Rather than fearing scarcity and limits, cornucopians argued that human progress meant unlimited prosperity. This approach was associated with a belief that technological development and market forces would abolish the Malthusian thesis of ecological degradation and resource depletion. Julian Simon claimed that human beings were the ultimate resource (Simon 1981). Rather than there being too many people the planet might have too few. Human beings are resourceful and can innovate, coming up with solutions. More humans mean more brains to think of better ways of addressing our collective problems. The market was seen by Simon as a major tool for resource conservation. If a resource was becoming scarce, its price would rise and this would encourage us to use substitutes. In turn if a resource, say oil, became more expensive, this would create an incentive to innovate.

Interestingly one of the Ostroms' students was a biographer of Julian Simon (Aligică 2007). Paul Dragos Aligică has also written a number of informative books on the Ostroms' work. It is obvious that Elinor Ostrom's work could be seen as fitting in with Simon's cornucopian analysis. Clearly while she believed human beings were imperfect she was optimistic, broadly, about our abilities. She certainly didn't think we were doomed to 'tragedy' or had to be forced into irrational outcomes like the prisoners in their dilemma. I think however that the technological optimism and faith in the market of Simon doesn't fit with her approach to ecology either. She was sceptical that a central plan would solve environmental problems but with her interest in the complexity of social and ecological systems, neither was she a *laissez faire* free-market environmentalist.

It would be simplistic to say that she was mid-point between the Malthusians and the free marketeers but her ideas do mean she potentially has an audience in both camps. I think her political ecology and indeed that of Vincent can be seen as based on management. Ecological problems can't just be left to the market for a variety of reasons but demand careful intervention. Forests, fisheries and other environments necessary for human prosperity have to be maintained in a sustainable way. They are not doomed to destruction, but markets may tend to promote short-term use rather than long-term conservation. Yet again it is worth making the point that her approach to ecology was based on problem solving. To summarise, she neither felt that we were doomed nor that we could leave ecology to the market. Careful construction of use rules would allow conservation.

Also in contrast to the pro-market approach to ecology, Elinor Ostrom promoted, as we have seen, a certain frugality. She noted in an interview in 2010:

> We need to get people away from the notion that you have to have a fancy car and a huge house. Some of the homes that have been built in the last 10 years just appal [sic] me. Why do humans need huge homes? I was born poor and I didn't know you bought clothes at anything but the Goodwill until I went to college. Some of our mentality about what it means to have a good life is, I think, not going to help us in the next 50 years. We have to think through how to choose a meaningful life where we're helping one another in ways that really help the Earth. (Elinor Ostrom, interview with Fran Korten in 2010 [Korten 2010])

While her approach would suggest that while she broadly concurred with green values such as non-violence, grassroots democracy and social justice/equality, such concern was only a starting point. All of these values or principles can be posed as problem or puzzle. Making a demand is very much a starting point. Non-violence, for example, is desirable but few Greens have been total pacifists, conflict resolution is necessary but, again, is difficult. Elinor Ostrom was almost obsessively concerned with commons problems but this focus meant that she constantly dealt with wider issues. On non-violence, she saw preventing war as another application of game theory and specifically the prisoner's dilemma. She was interested in the work of Robert Axelrod, to looking at how cooperation might develop and war be prevented. Trust and cooperation are necessary to promote peace and to help commoners to conserve, so were important to her. Ostrom's attempts to understand how to promote trust and cooperation are introduced in chapter seven.

Green politics, certainly in the UK, is increasingly concerned with intersectionality and difference, this is another area that fascinated Elinor and will be examined when we discuss her approach to feminism in chapter six. Equality has generally been a green demand and, along with her friend and fellow Nobel prize winning economist Amartya Sen, she was interested in how it might be promoted.

Elinor Ostrom wasn't interested in the politics of taking power but in the politics of negotiation necessary to democratically implement practical solutions to ecological problems. Equally she didn't see politics as a function of senates, parliaments, political parties or revolutionary groups alone. Politics, for her, was about governance and we all engage in governance in every part of our lives. Green politics from an Ostrom perspective would be about promoting self-governance not producing policies to be implemented from the centre. Ostrom focused on practical problem solving and saw effective problem solving as something akin to crowdsourcing. The many, not just a few experts, develop solutions that might work. It is interesting that in many ways Ostrom's perspectives seem up-to-date with the twenty-first century but were developed out of intellectual traditions that are twentieth century or earlier. Another area where she came up with innovative perspectives is economics, the subject of chapter four.

4

Beyond Markets and States

The financial crisis of 2008, the subsequent recession and continuing austerity have bred movements and candidates seeking to move beyond existing capitalism. The Occupy movement, new political parties like Podemos in Spain and radical candidates like Bernie Sanders in the United States and UK Labour Party leader Jeremy Corbyn are signs of change. There is an increasing awareness that mainstream economics fails to explain how our society works and how to solve problems such as ecological degradation and increasing inequality. Capitalism is increasingly criticised as a failed economic system. It is worth looking at the possible contribution Elinor Ostrom's work might make to those who seek alternatives to capitalism.

ECONOMIC ALTERNATIVES

While Elinor Ostrom did not set out to redesign or transform economics I think a careful study of her work helps those who seek to do so. It may be useful to distinguish economics, markets and neoliberalism to understand how her approach might be useful to those of us who want to see a different kind of economic system. Certainly, there is widespread criticism of the current capitalist economy from both those of us on the left and even from critics on the right. In focusing on the problem of cooperatively managing the commons, Ostrom shed some light on these fundamentals. The sociologist Jon Elster has argued:

> neoclassical economics will be dethroned if and when satisficing theory and psychology join forces to produce a simple and robust explanation of aspiration levels, or sociological theory comes up with a simple and robust theory of the relation between social norms and instrumental rationality. Until this happens, the

continued dominance of neoclassical theory is ensured by the fact that one can't beat something with nothing. (Elster 1986: 26–27)

Elster is arguing that until we replace the assumptions of mainstream economics that human beings are basically selfish and seek to maximise personal gain, an alternative economics will fail to provide an understanding of how humans work.

I think while she is not alone in doing so, Elinor Ostrom went a long way in providing such an alternative and has helped to challenge the certainties of economic orthodoxy. In seeking to understand how human cooperation could be promoted to conserve the commons, she helped provide the basis of an alternative theory of human motivation that challenges conventional economics in a fundamental way.

As has already been suggested, Elinor Ostrom wasn't an anti-capitalist. It might even be argued that she was a strongly pro-market thinker. Certainly, she and Vincent saw markets as a generally efficient way of distributing private goods and services. Her scepticism about the state didn't make her a free-market anarchist or a libertarian but she did tend to feel that state action often created unintended consequences and failures. Both she and Vincent were members of the Public Choice Society, which might reflect a strongly free-market approach. Public choice, an approach developed by the right-wing economist James Buchanan, argued that politicians were self-interested and used their positions to retain power rather than to serve the public good. Buchanan's public choice approach helped inspire right-wing pro-market political leaders like Margaret Thatcher and Ronald Reagan. Equally, even if Ostrom had advocated anti-capitalism, she would have argued that such a position could not be tested without a huge amount of research.

However, the kind of detailed research she undertook into human cooperation gives those of us who want a more cooperative and collective economy some inspiration. Neoliberalism is based on particular institutions and Elinor Ostrom's institutional analysis might help it to be understood more effectively. It is important to briefly describe the assumptions of mainstream economics and neo-liberalism before describing how Ostrom's work might help us move beyond them.

Like the 'tragedy of the commons', the very notion of economics is used to shut down debates on tackling inequality and other social ills. Economists suggest that their discipline is a science and it provides an accurate account of human behaviour, which proves that we are self-interested, competitive and largely disregard the needs of others. Capitalism is seen as the only viable economic system and alternatives are dismissed as naive. While Ostrom was not an anti-capitalist, we have already seen her rejection of any one panacea, she saw economic systems as diverse. Her work on the commons also suggests that while we may be self-interested, we can, if we get the institutional support right, come together and cooperate for the benefit of all.

Economics is derived from the Greek term 'oikos', which means 'household'; it is the same root as the 'eco' in ecology. Economics is essentially about welfare maximisation given limits and scarcity. By welfare, economists mean human well-being, so intrinsically economics isn't about profit making or how businesses grow but attempts to study how the whole of humanity can gain a better life. Economics has been defined as how scarce resources can be used to meet unlimited human wants. Economists generally assume that resources, such as land to build factories, raw materials to make into products as varied as yoghurt and motorbikes, and human labour, are finite. Thus our collective ability to produce goods is limited; we cannot make enough to provide for all our needs. As there is never enough to satisfy our wants, choices have to be made. Economics tends to focus on rationing and choice. Economic issues such as inflation or unemployment are part of a much wider picture.

Economics has become a largely mathematical discipline. It is assumed that while subjective wants cannot be directly measured, monetary values can be found and calculated. Economics employs a positivist method, positivism being the idea that only that which can be measured is worth studying.

Generally, economists have recognised two mechanisms for dealing with the linked problems of welfare, scarcity and resource allocation. These, of course, are markets and states. The fact that Ostrom focused on economics beyond markets and states probably cements her description as radical even if we ignore her other potential contributions. Markets are seen as providing a means of determining what to produce and who will get what is produced. Markets, working by exchange of goods and services which are priced with money, are understood to be generally efficient by economists. Where markets fail, the state is brought in. Most economists prefer markets because they feel that states are inefficient at dealing with our economic needs.

Many of those who agree with the assumption that markets generally work well are critical of the recent evolution of our global economy. Many thinkers and some activists have seen capitalism as distinct and inferior to the market, or if they favour capitalism in general have described the current system as a form of crony capitalism. The US activist David Korten is a populariser of this notion that markets work fairly well and even promote green values such as ecological sustainability, democracy and equality. However, he believes that capitalism is like a cancer, an unnatural growth of a healthy competitive system that leads to monopoly power with huge corporations putting competitors out of business, wrecking the environment, pushing down pay and impoverishing communities (Korten 1995). Much ink has been used to critique this kind of view, supporters of capitalism point to its virtues while Marxists, in contrast, and others on the left suggest that markets are flawed in many ways and tend to grow into monopoly. In turn, Austrian economists like Hayek enthusiastically support the market, but believe monopolies which damage competition are created by governments through regulation and licensing arrangements.

The present economic system is increasingly termed neoliberal by critics on the left. Liberal, in that it is based on market values, but new in the sense that corporate power is increasingly produced by government intervention. There is cooperation between large firms and the state, and states produce policies that favour firms such as reducing environmental regulations or cutting corporation tax. Government services are increasingly outsourced to private corporations. Critics argue that the profit of monopolistic firms, rather than the needs of people in general, motivates government action. In turn, more and more areas of life are commodified and seen as economic, for example, health is increasingly being opened up to market forces, and education is focused on business values.

Critics of economics, markets and neoliberalism can often see effects that they dislike, but supporters of capitalism argue that the positive effects outweigh the negative. In turn, even if we do see the negative effects as more significant, how do we create an alternative? A starting point perhaps is to examine some of the failings of economics as a discipline and look at human economic behaviour in a more nuanced and sophisticated way. This is exactly what Ostrom achieved.

She challenged the model of economic man or woman at the heart of economics and neoliberalism. We are far from being rational, selfish maximisers, as economists seem to assume. She agreed with the economist Herbert Simon that rather than maximising consumption our economic behaviour is about satisficing (Simon 1955). Simon argued that human beings can't make completely rational decisions to maximise our personal benefit, because we would need to be super computers to make all the necessary calculations. So he suggested that we satisfice, doing enough to gain satisfaction where possible, because the assumption that we maximise is unrealistic. Elinor also felt that economics has a generally unsophisticated take on human motivation and psychology, that instead of having one overwhelming need for material goods and services, we tend to have quite diverse needs. This insight, while obvious to many people, is a useful challenge to conventional economic assumptions.

She noted that economists generally believe that 'The rational strategy for such an individual in every situation is to maximize expected utility. While utility was originally conceived of as a way of combining a diversity of external values on a single internal scale, in practice, it has come to be equated with one externalized unit of measure – such as expected profits' (Ostrom 2010a: 3).

As we have seen, she also illustrated that human cooperation was possible. If cooperation is possible, then two interesting assumptions can be drawn from this. Firstly, commentators on the right would note that this means that we don't automatically need state intervention to solve our problems, as we are capable of dealing with them directly through grassroots cooperation. From the left, it also illustrates that a more cooperative collective economy is possible. Ostrom felt that human beings, given our diverse needs and goals, gained satisfaction from helping others. She warned that, while we should not move from complete pessimism to utter optimism, potentially cooperative and sharing economic behaviour was possible. We can't just assert that human beings are cooperative, but what Ostrom did was to look at how we could encourage more cooperative behaviour. Her discussion of cooperation and trust is examined in more detail in chapter seven. Clearly, if alternatives to neoliberalism are to be evolved, they have to work in a practical way which means promoting cooperation. The left and anti-capitalists have generally ignored this problem; Ostrom researched it in some detail.

Another core feature of her economics is that she moves beyond markets and states. It is however a gross simplification to say that she simply sees commons as a third alternative. Likewise, she doesn't see commons as a solution in all circumstances. She is not radically critical of either the state or the market but she does see a whole kaleidoscope of alternatives beyond them. The assumption that there is no alternative, and we have to put up with the present economic order, is utterly challenged by her work. Once we start seeing a variety of different forms of governance and economic institutions, we are open to the possibility of alternatives that potentially could transform social and economic reality in a positive direction.

The notion that economics extends beyond both the market and the state helps us deal with ecological issues. It is also important in a world where, from 3D printing to the World Wide Web, economic activity that is not covered entirely by the traditional contrast between the market and the state is growing fast. The notion of non-market non-state economic activity is missing from most forms of economic analysis, but Elinor Ostrom researched it as living reality. Her Nobel Prize lecture was entitled 'Beyond Markets and States: Polycentric Governance of Complex Economic Systems' (Ostrom 2010a). This ability, while accepting markets and states, to nonetheless move beyond them, makes her work unusual, relevant and exciting to all who challenge economic orthodoxies

It is worth remembering that rather than making broad ideological statements, which surprisingly or not is often the fashion of both mainstream economists and anti-capitalist critics, she poses issues as problems and then tries to solve them. I think this especially useful for creating economic alternatives that move us beyond neoliberalism. If we feel neoliberalism has failed, we should look at why alternatives might seem impossible. Strange as this may sound, it was very much Ostrom's technique. She saw common pool resources as a problem and a challenge. She noted that collective solutions were dismissed as impossible and then worked with great effort and imagination to show why this was not the case. We need to put the same kind of energy into examining potential alternatives that work.

Typically, we might note that more democratic forms of economic ownership are desirable. We could then, in an Ostrom fashion, note that such economic democracy may be difficult to achieve. In theory, economists might argue that it is impossible and that only private ownership is practical. However, there has been a wide variety of forms of economic democracy, including workers' control which also covers cooperatives. The diversity of forms of economic democracy could be studied, with examples which have succeeded and others that have failed. This would then allow the description of possible design rules for successful economic democracy, like the design rules for a working common. Such research could make use of the ideas and inspiration of workers and feedback conclusions. Where new left movements have had some electoral success, legal changes might be introduced to promote such forms of economic democracy.

ECONOMIC DEMOCRACY

Interestingly, while economists advocate private ownership, an increasingly important economic institution is the corporation. While seen as an engine of injustice, it is easily forgotten that the corporation is a collective entity. Indeed, Elinor Ostrom has suggested that the corporation is a commons, a view echoed by the autonomist Marxist theorists Hardt and Negri. So, another route to a different kind of economy might be to promote corporations as a form of economic democracy. While this might sound a very long shot, counter intuitive and even damaging, it is worth noting that formal economics struggles to see economics beyond individual ownership. Corporations could be owned by a whole society, and in Sweden trade unionists developed the Meidner plan, where pension funds would be used to buy corporations and then organise them as social rather than profit run institutions. Corporations might be seen to be simply too large to make democratic. Lenin argued that monopoly capitalism would create the conditions for revolution and corporations could be socialised to create a communist society.

Ostrom was an institutional economist. She observed from workers' cooperatives to small business to corporations, economic activity is based on particular institutions. Institutions can be conceptualised as sets of rules. This opens up the possibility of detailed institutional design as a means of creating a different kind of economy. Such institutional analysis has been off of the agenda or even simply unthought of by many on the left. There is a strong argument to say that Elinor was wrong to focus on this, and that large-scale social and political forces shape society. Marxists would argue that in a capitalist society, the economy acts as a kind of force field that crushes alternatives or co-opts them. The counter argument is that even if fundamental revolutionary change occurs, if little or no thought has been put into alternatives, capitalist institutions will quickly reassert themselves. In winning support for an alternative to neoliberalism, some thought as to the structure of alternatives needs to be presented.

Economics, as well as having a rather limited understanding of human motivation and institutions, is increasingly criticised for its methodological limitations. Economists rely on formal models and statistics; these provide a limited understanding of human behaviour. Elinor Ostrom did not reject either such formal modelling or the mathematics involved in economics, however she felt that such approaches were limited. From experiments to anthropology to historical case studies, she knew that more sophisticated and diverse research tools were necessary to make economics more rigorous and useful. Her approach to research methodology is another radical aspect of her work and is discussed in chapter eight.

Critics argue that she looked at small scale collective systems where individuals could learn to trust each other because they were in face to face contact. Collective ownership on a wider scale is viewed as utopian and unrealistic. However, as we have noted, this may be incorrect; not only are corporations collective entities but technological change is creating new opportunities for collective economic activity. For example, the evolution of the web has made social cooperation a powerful force even on a global level. The existence of Wikipedia is a sound illustration of an Ostrom approach. If we see Wikipedia as an encyclopedia, we can contrast its cooperative, crowd-sourced approach with the previous models. Previously we might have thought that only a profit-seeking company could publish an encyclopedia or we might suggest that some kind of government committee could produce one. Elinor Ostrom explicitly saw the web as providing the basis of a new knowledge economy based on sharing. Although she didn't undertake serious research in this area, she also saw cooperatives as potentially economically useful. Indeed, she wrote in support of the Grassroots Economic Organizing, a campaign site dedicated to 'Catalyzing workers co-ops and the solidarity economy' (www.geo.coop/node/647).

She notes the importance of collective economic activity based on individuals who can cooperate and suggests that the notion that 'individuals will not engage in collective action unless they are paid in some concrete fashion or are required to do so by well-enforced rules and laws' is false. Diverse, community based economics is possible, she suggests, but won't happen without good research and relevant practice. She and indeed Vincent Ostrom found that human motivation was diverse.

> When one assumes that individuals seek multiple goals including short-term self interest as well as longer term self and group interests, fairness, reciprocity, and achievement of community goals that are of importance to an individual and to others, it is more difficult to make simple predictions about behavior. One cannot simply switch from a presumption that no one will cooperate while engaged in purely voluntary activities, to assume that when groups of individuals learn how to trust one another, engage in reciprocity, discuss common goals, and work together to achieve these goals, they will always engage in collective action. (www.geo.coop/node/647)

She concluded her Nobel Prize lecture by noting how, over a lifetime, she had come to challenge the mainstream economic assumptions of universal self-interest and maximising behaviour:

The most important lesson for public policy analysis derived from the intellectual journey I have outlined here is that humans have a more complex motivational structure and more capability to solve social dilemmas than posited in earlier rational-choice theory. Designing institutions to force (or nudge) entirely self-interested individuals to achieve better outcomes has been the major goal posited by policy analysts for governments to accomplish for much of the past half century. Extensive empirical research leads me to argue that instead, a core goal of public policy should be to facilitate the development of institutions that bring out the best in humans. We need to ask how diverse polycentric institutions help or hinder the innovativeness, learning, adapting, trustworthiness, levels of cooperation of participants, and the achievement of more effective, equitable, and sustainable outcomes at multiple scales. (Ostrom 2010a: 24–25)

Elinor Ostrom's contribution to economics is useful to radicals in a number of ways. She gently subverts many of the foundations of mainstream economics by engaging with them. She indicates that the market and the state are not the only alternatives possible. Her exploration of property rights suggests that alternatives can be deepened and that economic explanations taken as common sense can be subverted. Perhaps most vitally, her method of research and assumptions about institutions can be used to investigate how alternatives can be made to work. Though Ostrom was not an anti-capitalist, creating alternatives to neoliberalism could fit with her emphasis on diversity, democracy and greater human cooperation. In turn, as a political economist she felt that economics cannot be separated easily from politics. To understand her contribution, we need to engage with her ideas about politics and her advocacy of deep participatory democracy. This is the subject of our next chapter.

5

Deep Democracy

One area where Elinor Ostrom was strikingly radical was in her support for deep and, where possible, direct democracy. She felt that the more power people had to make decisions that affected their lives the better such decisions were likely to be. Politics, for her, runs through human life. She saw politics as fundamentally about making decisions in cooperation with others. Politics was not just about parliaments, senates and political parties but about our everyday interactions with each other. Working out how to decide how to share the cooking, cleaning and washing up duties in a student flat is politics from her perspective. While she specifically focused on how commoners could agree to share out responsibility for conserving the commons, her general point is that politics can be used to describe human decision making in general. In turn, all politics is likely to be improved by participation.

Elinor Ostrom rejected managerialism and hierarchical systems of politics. She was sceptical of socialism if the term was associated with state power rather than popular participation. Typically, when asked if she would challenge descriptions of her work as 'socialist', she replied:

> Yes. I don't think they are supporting socialism as a top-down theory. A lot of socialist governments are very much top-down and I think my theory does challenge that any top-down government, whether on the right or the left, is unlikely to be able to solve many of the problems of resource sustainability in the world. (Ostrom 2009b)

Statism is often associated with socialist politics but many on the left are sceptical of states and promote popular participation instead of top-down command. For example, Michael Hardt and

Antonio Negri, often seen as autonomist or postmodern Marxists, are strong advocates of the commons (Hardt and Negri 2000). They note that statism is far from being a sign of radicalism and call for a new participatory society based on full democratic participation. Marx called for the 'withering away of the state' and was also a keen advocate of the commons. The state can act to protect those with wealth and power and manipulate rules to promote self-interest rather than the common good. Ostrom did not make grandstanding polemical statements but instead looked at specific problems and puzzles. However, her demand for ever-deeper democracy and greater participation is obvious. Her understanding of politics is very different from most political scientists.

This reflects her perspective on the commons. The tragedy of the commons, and the other formal models that overlap with it, suggested that individuals cannot succeed in coming together to make collective decisions that conserve resources. It is assumed as a result of these models that we humans are incompetent so we need someone else to take care of us. The state or the market fill in, because of the free-rider problem we will disrupt the commons but if the commons is put in the private hands of an individual, or the state takes control, the problem can be solved. The state can tell us what to do and private ownership eliminates the need to work with others to conserve the commons. Ostrom rejected this view that humans cannot cooperate and the commons is doomed to degradation and eventual collapse.

States are made of people, so if people are flawed so are states. It is simplistic to identify a problem and demand that the state solves the problem. Ostrom specifically felt that states might destroy the ability of commoners to maintain their commons. There is a knowledge problem with the state, states may employ experts who have little knowledge of local situations. This perspective is drawn from the right-wing economist Friedrich Hayek. Most economists argue that for an economy to work well, economic agents such as consumers and firms must have adequate knowledge. The closer an economy is to a state of perfect knowledge the more efficiently it will work. Hayek, in contrast, argued that knowledge is always imperfect. In an economy there are billions of individual decisions to be made, so the state will never be able to plan an economy because it lacks the knowledge to do so. Markets are imperfect but as they are decentralised, they are better for Hayek in overcoming this knowledge problem (Hayek 1937).

Ostrom disagreed with Hayek when he seemed to reject all planning; she did not think that the market was a perfect solution but she agreed with him that states might lack the knowledge to make good decisions. While this perspective might be associated with a right-wing view point and echoes thinkers like the free-market economists, it can also be seen as an aspect of a left politics. Elinor Ostrom was strongly critical, for example, of colonialism and neo-colonialism, which amongst many crimes viewed the communities it dominated as incompetent. Too often she felt that the state was viewed as a 'black box'. There is a problem and we simply demand that the state does something about it. It is naively felt that the state will take the correct action and the problem will be solved.

She felt that as well as the state being an imperfect institution and beyond ideological support for deep democracy, there were strong practical reasons for promoting self-governance. In the commons, local people often have a better understanding of the problems they face and possible solutions than a government far away. Also, if the problems of the tragedy of the commons are to be overcome this may demand some sacrifices. An individual may graze fewer cattle or catch fewer fish in the short term so as to make sure that the commons remains productive and green in the long term. If individuals have a say in how the rules of sacrifice are made they are more likely to abide by them, than if the rules are made without their input or even consent.

Ostrom believed that were a variety of roles for the state but that viewing the state as a natural force for good was naive. Her view was that democracy was not, as noted, to be found only in formal structures such as parliaments, but ran through the whole of society. In our daily lives we interact with others and constantly come to agreement through negotiations; these are deeply political.

Human beings potentially can self-govern rather than defer to the state:

Using a broader theory of rationality leads to potentially different views of the state. If one sees individuals as helpless, then the state is the essential external authority that must solve social dilemmas for everyone. If, however, one assumes individuals can draw on heuristics and norms to solve some problems and create new structural arrangements to solve others, then the image of what a national government might do is somewhat different. There is a very considerable role for large-scale governments, including national defense, monetary policy, foreign policy, global trade policy, moderate redistribution, keeping internal peace when some groups organize to prey on others, provision of accurate information and of arenas for resolving conflicts with national implications, and other large-scale activities. But national governments are too small to govern the global commons and too big to handle smaller scale problems. (Ostrom 1998: 17)

As we noted in the previous chapter, the narrow economic conception of human rationality, indicates that we are too self-interested to easily work with others. For Ostrom a broader rationality included the insight that we were not purely selfish but might in many circumstances gain satisfaction from helping others. This opens up the possibility of cooperation and self-governance, which if supported by appropriate structures, can create more democratic systems. However, as the passage above suggests she saw a role for the state in various areas of human life.

Thus democracy for Elinor Ostrom was about people shaping the rules that govern our lives, not simply about delegating power to a minority of people to make the rules. This perspective fits in with what might be seen as a form of radical republicanism or self-government. Republicanism, not to be confused with the right-wing US party of that name, is derived from a Latin term 'Res publica' which refers to public things. It can be traced back to classical Greek ideas of direct democracy or the creation of medieval city states.

In contrast, politics in the twenty-first century is increasingly seen as top-down management in a neoliberal system. This means that levels of discontent rise and are often exploited by right-wing populists. Such populism, rather than seeking to give control to the people, is used to place right-wing politicians in power, the election of Donald Trump as US President being just one example of a worldwide trend. Thus a cycle of ever receding democracy seems apparent in society. An Ostrom approach of promoting self-government provides a radical and attractive alternative.

Ostrom believed that we needed education for democracy, so we could learn about the promise and pitfalls of self-governance. Her radical idea of democracy meant that her conception of politics was often marginalised or rejected. In turn, a political party offering radical democracy is perhaps a contradiction in terms. Deep democracy or self-government is not a slogan that can be automatically introduced. In 2016 the Pirate Party has gained parliamentary seats on a platform of participatory democracy and advocates the commons. In Spain the new left party Podemos has gained votes with similar policies. In Latin America, governments in states like Venezuela and Ecuador have advocated collective grassroots democratic control.

As I write, the practical implication of such democratic control has proved difficult. Critics of the Latin American left governments argue that they have not proved working alternatives, their supporters point to disruption by right-wing forces. The Occupy movement, Arab Spring and other protest movements haven't even managed to gain enough power to be seen to fail.

In a society where top-down rules are standard, we have little or no experience of how to build democratic self-governing structures that work. It would be too pessimistic to argue that the aspirations of the Pirates are unrealistic, however without close attention to how to construct new structures, aspiration is unlikely to be translated into effective workable systems. Ostrom's whole body of research, while focused on the commons, promotes generalised democratic control. Again, it is not enough to be for something, for ecology or direct democracy, the point is to pose this demand as a puzzle or problem and then to look at ways of better answering the question posed.

Marx and Engels looked to the withering away of the state and direct control of society by human beings. They explored macro issues of social class, historical development, technology and other issues, to create a powerful body of theory. What Ostrom provides in contrast to those of us on the left in is an emphasis on the micro mechanism of promoting democratic control. Simply moving from authoritarian and class-based societies to more democratic and equal societies may be impossible, unless we attend to this analysis. Vincent Ostrom stated on many occasions that he was sympathetic to the Marxist wish to see a 'withering away of the state', however he was sceptical that Marxism could lead to self-governance without a detailed consideration of how this could be achieved in practice (V. Ostrom 1997: 83). If we are familiar with systems where self-governance is rare and participation in formal politics is slight, it will be difficult to move to a deeper democracy. A theme that emerges from Elinor Ostrom's work is that while particular principles, including deep democracy, may be desirable, these can only be put into practice with careful preparation.

So how did she believe that self-governance could work in practice? For a start, she suggests we should reject utopian blueprints. She also stressed the importance of an emphasis on constructing rules. In politics we pick a side; in contrast, for Ostrom the main emphasis was to participate in creating rules and, in effect, constitutions. She and Vincent saw this as a material practical task. Demystifying politics is important. The more we understand how rules and institutions work, the more transparent the exercise of power is. By making politics less mysterious, participation is easier and change, while difficult, may be possible.

The Ostroms made their own furniture and helped build their own home. Building political structures to some extent is directly analogous to this. According to Vincent both are forms of human artisanship, where individuals work with materials to construct artefacts to improve human life (V. Ostrom 1980).

Diversity is also important for a working form of deep democracy. Democracy perhaps isn't really all that democratic if it simply means rule by a majority; democratic systems need to provide space for minority opinions. This is another reason why the Ostroms focused more on negotiation than questions of taking political power. Winning is not the key problem for them in politics, providing a way of giving different voices space is. Not only is this a classic political dilemma, but positively, if diversity can be respected and worked with, it has a practical benefit. Decisions are more likely to be good if they are tested and face scrutiny from those with differing viewpoints. The assumption that commons and collective decision-making work best when a society is homogenous was not promoted by Ostrom. Individuals inevitably have different interests, there are likely to be diverse group identities. Creating systems that harness the creativity of diverse views should be a key political goal. This seems to reflect the view of the political theorist Chantal Mouffe that democracy is agonistic. Agonism is the principle of dialogue between those with different opinions, which Mouffe views as vital.

Mouffe notes, using a terminology, similar to that of Elinor and Vincent Ostrom that difference has to be acknowledged in developing democratic systems:

> We can therefore reformulate our problem by saying that envisaged from the perspective of 'agonistic pluralism' the aim of democratic politics is to transform antagonism into agonism. This requires providing channels through which collective passions will be given ways to express themselves over issues, which, while allowing enough possibility for identification, will not construct the opponent as an enemy but as an adversary. An important difference with the model of 'deliberative democracy', is that for 'agonistic pluralism', the prime task of democratic politics is not to eliminate passions from the sphere of the public, in order to render a rational consensus possible, but to mobilize those passions towards democratic designs. (Mouffe 2000: 16)

The Ostrom approach to democracy also has similarities with the US radical thinker, associated with social ecology, Murray Bookchin. He was also inspired by city states and promoted the idea of municipal confederalism.

> My concern is to see that the municipal level act as a brake upon the centralization of the state and ultimately lead to the abolition of the centralized state in a free municipal confederation of towns and cities and villages structured in a libertarian form.
>
> You know this is an ideal that is ages old. It belonged to the early Swiss confederacy, not the present one. It was an ideal that existed in New England. Farmers in New Hampshire and Vermont and the

upper valley tried to establish a republic of towns and cities during the American Revolution. (Bookchin 1986: 8)

Bookchin's ideas, in turn, have inspired the construction of a post-state political system based on participatory democracy in Rojava. Rojava, the autonomous mainly Kurdish area in Northern Syria, threw out the Assad government in a revolution in 2011. Despite having to fight the so-called Islamic State, they have attempted to build a deep democracy. To overcome potential sectarian conflict, different communities, including Arabs, Kurds, Armenians and Chechens share power. Typically, a small town might be co-governed by male and female figures from different ethnic communities.

The Kurdistan Workers Party (PKK) moved from a specifically Marxist-Leninist model based to one inspired by Bookchin. Their sister Party the People's Democratic Union (PYD) introduced the model into Syria. The PKK leader Ocalan stated,

> Democratic confederalism is the contrasting paradigm of the oppressed people. Democratic confederalism is a non-state social paradigm. It is not controlled by a state. At the same time, democratic confederalism is the cultural organisational blueprint of a democratic nation.

> Democratic confederalism is based on grassroots participation. Its decision making processes lie with the communities. Higher levels only serve the coordination and implementation of the will of the communities that send their delegates to the general assemblies. (https://corporatewatch.org/news/2016/apr/18/democratic-confederalism-kurdistan)

While discussion of the Rojava revolution would require a whole book and it is not without its critics who say it masks PYD control, it does seem to be a potential working example of an Ostrom like self-governing system.

> The commune is the base level of Rojava's council system. In general, communes are made up of 30–400 households in a city, or a whole village in the countryside. The entire population of the

commune meets every two weeks, and it elects a board. The board meets every week, and all members of the commune are able to attend board meetings if they wish. All posts must be filled by a male and female co-chair. All representatives are recallable by the membership of the commune.

We visited a Mala Gel, or people's house, run by Şehit Hozan commune in Amude in Rojava's Cizîrê canton, where we spoke to the commune's male co-chair. Şehit Hozan commune represents 400 families in their neighbourhood who vote for the board of the commune. We were told that the commune has commissions dealing with services, economy, Kurdish language teaching, organising lectures, self-defence, reconciliation and justice.

The commune's reconciliation and justice commission tries to resolve problems that arise between members of the commune. For example, we were told that the commission had recently been asked to mediate when someone was injured in a road traffic accident and when there had been a dispute about land ownership. We were told that often the commission is able to resolve these disputes. (https://corporatewatch.org/news/2016/apr/18/democratic-confederalism-kurdistan)

While diversity and difference are beneficial, Elinor Ostrom argued that if there was consensus around the constitutional basics of a self-governing system, this was helpful. If we are contributing to rules that we agree to, we are more likely to accept being on the losing side of an argument. However, the difficult issue of minority representation remains. If one viewpoint is consistently defeated, they will lose their respect for a system of governance. Minority rights, difference and the need to negotiate are important questions, relevant at multiple scales from a commons up to a state.

Education for democracy is also essential for self-governance. Elinor Ostrom argued that political education was poor and to the limited extent that we are taught about politics in school this deals with parliaments, senates and even monarchs. Self-governance is more likely to thrive and grow if we are taught about how to make decisions, construct potential rules and negotiate with others from an early age. Any revolution is likely to continue the previous undemocratic systems if it fails to look to educating us in democracy and learning how to create deep direct democracy.

Democracy is about power and one aspect of power relations which is often forgotten is gender. Elinor Ostrom, while she did not undertake detailed research into gender, can be conceptualised as a feminist thinker. Ostrom's emphasis on diversity equally aligns her with an intersectional approach long before the word was commonly used. Intersectionality is the notion that oppression has more than one dimension, typically intersectional feminists would suggest that gender, class, ethnicity, age, health and other factors can both cause oppression and intersect in doing so. Elinor Ostrom's potential relevance to feminism and intersectionality is examined in the next chapter.

6

Feminism and Intersectionality

'I got circled in the schoolroom, out on the playground.'

'You Jew! You Jew!' she recalled, her voice rising, imitating the taunts. 'Having that experience as a kid and being a woman, and having that challenge as it has been at different times to be a woman, I've got pretty good sympathy for people who are not necessarily at the centre of civic appreciation.'

(Elinor Ostrom interviewed by Leonard 2009)

The politics of difference and liberation were central to Elinor Ostrom, however, they came from her particular perspective which is both illuminating and a little unusual. She was an advocate of difference and plurality, who strongly believed in promoting women and minorities. Equally, while keen to see how biology might influence society and vice versa, she was a strongly anti-essentialist thinker who, far from seeing nature as fixed, was aware of its changing characteristics. Such anti-essentialism chimes with other theorists who have advocated ecological politics and feminist commitment such as Donna Haraway. Elinor Ostrom's work also fits into a larger feminist economics which has challenged the discipline for being male biased and naive in terms of its basic research methods and assumptions. She rarely made specific statements about feminism but it imbues her thinking, which moved away from experts, generally male, to a method that promote listening and participation.

As we have seen, Elinor Ostrom's life experience made her strongly supportive of the promotion of diversity. It is highly instructive to remember that she was the first woman to win the Nobel Prize for economics when she was awarded it in 2009. Women may have had the vote in many countries for over a century, but economics remains a male club. Economics is largely mathematised and women born in the 1930s like Elinor Ostrom may have had less opportunity to study mathematics at school, immediately shutting down access. Elinor Ostrom generally focused on the micro level and she noted that she was taught methodological individualism, the idea that society is made up of sovereign individuals, not social classes or other groups. For both reasons she might be seen as ignoring power and structural influences on human behaviour. Nonetheless, notions of power and contestation run right through her work. It was obvious to her that in the 1950s and 1960s white men had more power in the USA than other identities. From an early age she did what she could to promote diversity. Working in Boston in recruitment to support her first husband through law school, she was proud to try to promote a less homogenous work force.

> When I returned to Los Angeles in 1957 and applied for a professional position in the Personnel Office at UCLA, I was greatly relieved to learn that I had received a strong recommendation from my Boston employer. This was particularly gratifying because I had been able to diversify the firm's staff, previously all white and Protestant or Catholic, to include several new employees who were black or Jewish. (Ostrom 2010b: 3).

Elinor Ostrom did not engage directly in either political activity around feminism and anti-racism or make direct academic contributions in these field. Her research focused, as has been seen, on the commons. She used exhaustive research to find out more and was reluctant to comment outside her area of expertise. Nonetheless some of her theoretical assumptions are useful, I feel, for promoting a politics of diversity. A key concept she and Vincent Ostrom promoted was polycentricism. Polycentricism means many centred. Political scientists, managers, politicians and others in the 1950s and 1960s generally assumed that one central authority with a chain of linear command was the most efficient form of administration. US politics, with its messy and overlapping structures of authority including a federal government, states, cities and local governments within cities and states, was seen as inefficient. Along with an increasing trust in experts, technology and modernism, monocentricism was seen as vital to social progress.

In contrast, Elinor and Vincent argued that diverse forms of political authority were surprisingly beneficial. The concept of polycentricism is shared with the philosopher Michael Polanyi. His argument is that knowledge is produced and science advances when different perspectives are allowed free play. Diversity leads to intellectual strength. While knowledge is incomplete for a particular central authority and will lead to policy failure, decentralisation and diversity lead to better understanding. We normally assume that uniformity leads to social cohesion and that diversity is somehow threatening. Paul Dragos Aligică, a former student of Elinor and Vincent, has argued in detail that the Ostrom's celebration of diversity is a radical break from most other thinkers (Aligică 2014). Citing Habermas as an example, he notes that often a thinker will accept diversity but look for some at first hidden unity that can be produced, transforming difference back into uniformity and supposed cohesion.

While Elinor Ostrom would argue that diversity might in some circumstances be a weakness; as we have seen she stressed looking at the context rather than making broad-brush assumptions; but she generally saw it as something of great value. The implicit point here and one reflected in her statements is that a society is made up of very diverse groups and that instead of seeing this as a problem, we should see it as something beneficial. Minorities are attacked as damaging because they threaten uniformity. In contrast, contemporary feminists are increasingly embracing intersectionality, viewing sources of oppression as diverse and interlocking rather than seeing, for example, racism as more dangerous than sexism or class inequality. Intersectionality might be seen as a form of polycentricism.

This also links to Ostrom's anti-essentialism. Anti-essentialism is the rejection of the idea of an unchanging and permanent characteristic that establishes an identity. For example, an essentialist understanding of human nature might claim that human beings have intrinsic features such as competitive behaviour. Anti-essentialism is often seen as subversive of any kind of radical political commitment. Those critical of anti-essentialism see it as linked to anti-foundationalism. Instead of defending particular values as a foundation for political action, values are seen in context and may be subject to change. Anti-essentialism and anti-foundationalism have been criticised as promoting anything-goes forms of moral relativism. Much political philosophy rests on the search for foundations such as the pursuit of democracy and equality. Much debate centres on how to reconcile contradictions between apparently foundational political principles.

Critics of anti-essentialism argue that unchanging principles must be defended. They suggest that to engage in relativism or to say that we live in a world of flux and movement is to cut away all real political and moral choices. I would disagree! While Ostrom's anti-essentialism isn't immediately obvious, it is clearly part of her work, and whether you agree with it or not, certainly marks her out as an interesting thinker. Oddly, while Vincent Ostrom was derisive about Derrida and it might seem the Ostroms were distant from similar continental philosophers, the Ostroms' stress on language and criticism of fixed identities points to similarities with post-structuralist and postmodern thought.

Most obviously, rather than debating ideological principles in the abstract, Ostrom was interested to see what worked in practice. Like Marx she has a set of underlying political sympathies but the key point for both thinkers, different as they are in some respects, is what happens in material reality. Both were anti-utopian, rejecting blueprints but trying to understand how society works.

Generally, we look at political or economic debates including those around feminism, difference and intersectionality, as putting forward particular positions which are then fought over. While there are positions or principles or values that influence Elinor Ostrom, it was not her way to engage in a forceful for-or-against battle. Instead, as we have seen, she would pose a problem and work hard to come up with an answer. While she personally enjoyed debate, problem solving was what she emphasised. She was not looking for an essential and total solution to, say, ecological problems or inequality but kept these concerns in the background and was interested in a specific intervention in a particular context.

The debates around gender, ethnicity and other forms of difference often seem to search for fixed positions. The Ostrom approach is not only that difference is generally to be celebrated but the idea of a fixed, unchanging identity is unlikely. In turn, debates on feminism are too often haunted by a use of biology that is used to silence contending voices. A right-wing politics often argues that society is ultimately conditioned by nature, and nature in turn provides an essential foundation. There are numerous examples of such socio-biology, where nature is used to close down debate.

It is very clear that Ostrom has two contributions to this that are potentially rather subversive. She was aware that nature did matter, thus in her work on commons, she looked at how both social sciences and natural sciences could improve understanding. She did not, I feel, view nature as something fixed, foundational and unchanging. This is reflected in her reading of Ernst Mayr's history of biology. Mayr argues that a key barrier to the acceptance of the theory of evolution was essentialism (Mayr 1982). While religion which promoted a creationist perspective is usually seen as the main reason why evolution was rejected, Mayr notes that an essentialist analysis developed by Aristotle was more of a barrier. Aristotle argued that each species had its own essence which separated it from other species, a bear was utterly distinct from a badger, a snake from a snail. Difference was based on unchanging intrinsic factors. Essentialism made it impossible to conceive of evolution, because how could one distinct species change into another?

She observed that: 'Mayr argued that systems "almost always have the peculiarity that the characteristics of the whole cannot (not even in theory) be deduced from the most complete knowledge of the components, taken separately or in other partial combinations" (p. 63)' (Ostrom 2004: 44). Ostrom's anti-essentialism, together with her respect for both natural and social sciences, is unusual. It provides an alternative to approaches that see human beings as essentially social and thus separate from nature. It is also a good way of challenging biological arguments, usually, to be frank, based on dubious science, to license sexism or other exclusionary behaviour. Either we ignore the fact that we are part of nature, suggesting that as cultured beings with language we are separate, or we use biology to promote naïve notions about human nature. Malthus and Garrett Hardin suggest that human beings are part of nature and as such we will inevitably be prisoners of over population and disaster. Ostrom sees humanity as part of nature but is less pessimistic.

Post-structuralist and postmodernist feminism incorporate this opposition to essentialism and are also known for a turn toward language. Both Elinor and Vincent Ostrom noted the importance of language in shaping human social interactions. One of the best-known feminist thinkers in recent decades is Gayatri Chakravorty Spivak, a literary theorist, known for her translation of French philosopher Jacques Derrida's *Of Grammatology*. Spivak has suggested that there are multiple dimensions of oppression, with anti-colonial struggles failing to liberate peasant communities, or European feminists failing women in the south of the globe. In her essay 'Can the Subaltern Speak?' she suggests that postcolonial academics have reproduced oppression and the 'subaltern' such as a peasant is always silenced (Spivak 1988). Spivak has combined a commitment to liberation with an emphasis on language and diversity. Spivak was influenced by Derrida's deconstruction. Derrida argued that meaning was always slippery, so philosophy which uses words tends to deconstruct. We cannot easily produce analytical categories in philosophy because these are presented in words, and the meaning of a word is always deferred. He argued that precision in debate is always under threat. While deconstruction has been widely criticised, this basic point is of vital importance. We communicate using words but the precise meaning of a particular word may not be fixed or self-evident. Both Elinor and Vincent were aware that words shape social reality and can be open to varied interpretation.

In turn, Aligică has argued that Elinor Ostrom is both a pragmatist and that her pragmatism links to that of linguistic theory (Aligică 2014). Ostrom was aware of the influence of language on society, aware of the problems of simplified language and as we have seen committed to diversity. Her work also relates to that of Spivak because both reject Eurocentrism and stress the need to listen to diverse voices.

FEMINIST ECONOMICS

Elinor Ostrom's work also fits into a wider body of feminist economics. Economists generally argue that their work is gender neutral and neutral in terms of ethnicity, sexual preference, etc.

Feminist economists, despite differences on other matters, reject such neutrality and argue that traditional economics is methodologically flawed. Economists assume that they are neutral but as an often almost exclusively male body, ignore certain questions and include various unconscious biases. Economists have stressed factors that can easily be measured in monetary terms, looking at problems of formal employment and economic growth. Feminist economists argue that some of the influences on human well-being that are most important are ignored by mainstream economists. Veronika Bennholdt-Thomsen and Maria Mies (1999) have argued that the actual economy is like an iceberg. The top of the iceberg which is above water included the goods and services produced in an economy, measured by GDP. However, in the same way an iceberg is mainly below water and may not be immediately visible, the economy in terms of our general welfare is invisible, or at least, obscure to economists. Domestic labour, often carried out by women, such as caring for children, the sick and the elderly, is more vital than banking but is not measured. Much economic activity is subsistence, food is grown, especially by peasants in many parts of the world but is used directly and not measured. The iceberg also includes nature which is vital for human survival. The commons, of course, is associated to some extent with non-monetary informal economic activity.

Deidre McCloskey is a linguistically sophisticated feminist economist. As Donald McCloskey, prior to her transition, she focused on economic history and incidentally produced interesting research into medieval commons, suggesting that common fields brought benefits to the peasants who used them (McCloskey 1991). As Deidre, after her transition, she is known for combining support for free-market economics with a critique of much mainstream economic methodology, while campaigning on liberation issues, including freedom for Chelsea Manning, that might be seen as the prerogative of the left. Her postmodern economic feminism, while market based, argues that assumptions of traditional economic rationality are a mark of a male dominated and flawed discipline. She is highly critical of the notion of 'Max U alone', by this she means that it is too simplistic to say that humans always try to maximise utility.

Utility is the term economists use for personal material well-being
or benefit:

> Men and women behave (roughly) the same way in response to
> constraints, but the way is well captured for many problems by
> Max U alone. [. . .] My replies to the big questions can be summed
> up this way: the little boys' rules for economic behavior or science
> (Greed is Good; use only Max U; ignore the complexities of
> human character beyond pure prudence) are not what grown-ups,
> male or female, in life or science, actually practice. Feminism
> draws attention to the grown-up practices of the economy and of
> economics. (McCloskey 2000: 364)

McCloskey also provides an accessible and rather attractive account
of what is useful about postmodernism, challenging essentialism
with some clear words:

> People are always getting into quarrels about the Essential Meaning
> of X. Never mind that if 20th-century philosophy has taught us
> anything (there is some debate among critics of 20th-century
> philosophy) it is that meanings do not lie around like pebbles to
> be picked up but are social agreements, like definitions of the word
> 'hominid' or 'income'. Yet it is still the case that one of the most
> effective rhetorical devices is to define away your opponent with
> an Essential Meaning. You know the device. If someone defines
> what you do as 'not [Essentially] economics then she doesn't have
> to listen to you. Or answer your objections.' (2000: 363)

McCloskey's work is a good supplement to and has many parallels
with Ostrom's; neither fit neatly into preconceived categories.

Elinor's focus was not on the political economy of inflation or
finance but on fields, fisheries and irrigation systems. What she
saw as a vital problem, the governance of commons, was largely
ignored by other academics. Thus the kind of work she undertook
implicitly followed that of feminist economists who argue that much
of importance to women is invisible within the discipline. We can
see how it reflects McCloskey's feminist economics, challenging

conventional economics as a little naive, listening to people rather than using formal models as the only means of understanding reality and with reference to culture, linguistics and diverse meanings. Like McCloskey, her understanding of human motivation moves beyond the simplistic maximisation of utility and greed is good to a more nuanced perspective on our economic behaviour.

Elinor also argued in an interview with the academic journal *Feminist Economics* that she was 'very strongly influenced by the work of Amartya Sen. Sen has long stressed the importance of respect for others. In his imaginative and rigorous analysis' Sen has been conceptualised as a feminist economist, like Ostrom, using tools from conventional economics to move towards a more radical conception. Most dramatically, he argued that selective abortion and infanticide explained why 'More Than 100 Million Women Are Missing' (Sen 1990). He and Elinor were good friends, they did both tend to combine an interest in the free-market Austrian economist James Buchanan with an interest in themes such as equality and ecological sustainability.

Feminist economists have tended to argue that academics can be elitist and use their research to ignore the voices of non-academics. Elinor Ostrom argued that human liberation demanded that we rethink how we do research and how we educate others. She saw human beings as thoughtful and resourceful, fallible and imperfect but due respect. Elinor Ostrom can, in this regard, be seen as a feminist because of her notion of the co-production of knowledge, via academic engagement with a population, rather than simply developing formal models to then tell people what to do. Chapter eight describes her approach to intellectual work, research methodology and education.

While she did not see gender as central to her research, her wider analysis is instructive in promoting feminism and diversity. It is worth considering the challenges she found but was able to overcome in winning the economics Nobel. She told *Feminist Economics*:

In political science at UCLA, there had not been any women on the faculty or as graduate students for something like 40 years. In my entry class, there were four women out of a large class and a fair amount of controversy about this. Fortunately, I had some great fellow graduate students and kind of learned to overlook this type of discrimination.

[…] I do know a bit about the career of one other woman graduate student who was in my entry class. She did become so depressed over academic problems that she took a draft of her dissertation and burned it and moved out of academia entirely. (Ostrom in May and Summerfield 2012)

Politics is often seen as a matter of the oppressed overcoming the oppressors; feminists, for example, dismantling patriarchy. Ostrom was certainly keen to see women, minorities, peasants and workers win more influence however she was most interested in the politics of cooperation. The left, in its diversity, has argued that politics is about winning power, but once power is won, how can a cooperative society be built? This was an important area of research for Elinor Ostrom and is discussed in the next chapter.

7

Trust and Cooperation

The commons fail, ultimately, because distrust leads to a lack of cooperation. The 'tragedy' is based on formal models like the prisoner's dilemma that suggest that competitive behaviour will win out over cooperation and the commons will be destroyed. Thus, the commons problem can be seen as a problem of cooperation and trust. Elinor Ostrom did not believe in making sweeping statements about human nature; she did not believe that human beings were either basically cooperative or inevitably selfish, she was instead interested in how trust and cooperation could be nurtured to overcome the commons dilemmas and similar problems. This is an area of discussion that should be of great interest to those of us who we seek to promote a more cooperative and peaceful society. Often it is asserted that human nature shows we are intrinsically competitive by those on the right, or intrinsically cooperative by those on the left. Ostrom's approach was to reject such broad generalisations and her anti-essentialism made her suspicious of unchanging foundations of human behaviour. She also warned that cooperation wasn't always good; for example, if criminals cooperate they are better placed to do social harm.

Ostrom's approach to trust and cooperation was influenced strongly by the German game theorist Reinhard Selten. She noted:

In the fall of 1980, Vincent joined a year-long research effort called 'Guidance, Control, and Performance Evaluation in the Public Sector' at the Center for Interdisciplinary Research (ZiF), Bielefeld University [. . .]. This was an important event in both of our intellectual journeys. It was wonderful to be with academics from multiple disciplines [. . .] I was fortunate that Reinhard Selten invited me to join his game theory seminar on the Bielefeld campus. During long walks in the woods behind the campus, Reinhard and

I discussed an evolving framework for institutional analysis and the centrality of game theory to its development. (Ostrom 2010b: 11–12).

It is often forgotten that traditional economics assumes implicitly both competitive and cooperative behaviour. As we have noted, economists have tended to argue that human beings are self-interested. We want the best for ourselves as individuals and compete against others to achieve it. Adam Smith, in *The Wealth of Nations*, argued that the pursuit of personal gain led to the collective good; competition led to the creation of an efficient market that tended to bring benefits to all. A good illustration of the benefits of competition, according to traditional economists, is the operation of competition between firms. Firms are locked into battle, if they do not produce what consumers want they will go out of business. Firms are forced to be efficient, cutting costs so they can cut prices. Competition drives efficiency. Elinor Ostrom, while not disputing this, would argue that the short-term pursuit of profit might come at the expense of other values and would tend to destroy the commons. Marx argued that firms relied on the exploitation of workers' labour power, and competition produced winners who gained monopoly power. Nonetheless the example shows why economists have often favoured competition.

However, in the absence of cooperation and trust, a market based economy would soon fall apart. Firms need some measure of trust to do business. Too much competition would eventually destroy the system. An excellent example of this is the financial crisis of 2008. Banking is a risky business but banks can avoid crisis by lending to each other. Increasingly complex and virtually fraudulent investments reduced trust between banks, which meant that it was difficult to get credit at a time of crisis, and banks started to collapse. It is often forgotten that Adam Smith stressed cooperation and a range of other virtues, writing not only *The Wealth of Nations*, which promoted competition, but *The Theory of Moral Sentiments* that argued for a range of moral virtues including sympathy for others. He observed:

How selfish soever man [sic] may be supposed, there are evidently some principles in his nature, which interest him in the fortunes of others, and render their happiness necessary to him, though he derives nothing from it, except the pleasure of seeing it. Of this kind is pity or compassion, the emotion which we feel for the misery of others, when we either see it, or are made to conceive it in a very lively manner. That we often derive sorrow from the sorrow of others, is a matter of fact too obvious to require any instances to prove it, for this sentiment, like all the other original passions of human nature, is by no means confined to the virtuous and humane, though they perhaps may feel it with the most exquisite sensibility. The greatest ruffian, the most hardened violator of the laws of society, is not altogether without it. (Smith 2006: 3)

Ostrom's pursuit of cooperation is of interest to socialists who would like to see a society based on sharing but it is also vital to those who want to overcome crisis in a capitalist economy. The formal models used to suggest that the 'tragedy of the commons' was a threat, also provide a warning for traditional economists. Competitive behaviour, within limits, leads to shared prosperity, according to traditional economists. The prisoner's dilemma and tragedy of the commons suggests in contrast that competitive behaviour leads, via the Nash equilibrium, to a loss for all the players. If the two prisoners assume that each are rational and self-interested they both 'defect', this means they both confess, so they both get longer sentences than if they had both refused to confess. Rational economic actors following the logic of their situation are worse off than if they had been considerate of each other's needs. Although the prisoner's dilemma might seem a rare situation, it basically subverts Adam Smith's justification for self-interest. For Smith, self-interest leads to benefits for all; game theory hints that self-interest reduces benefits for all and usually means an individual is worse off than if they had cooperated with others.

Elinor Ostrom was interested in investigating how cooperation could be encouraged so that commons can be conserved. She posed the following question 'How do groups of individuals gain trust?' (Ostrom 2003: 19). The conventional interpretation of the prisoner's dilemma and tragedy of the commons is to suggest that trust which leads to cooperation is unlikely. This interpretation indicates that the government should be brought in or the commons privatised. Even if these policies were desirable, which we might doubt, they fail to account for situations where they would be unrealistic.

Elinor Ostrom suggested that what Hardin was outlining was a formal model, essentially a piece of economics. Economists generally like to construct such models based on formal logic, that take a situation based on human choice and represent it in an abstract form. The formalism loved by economists is often criticised for being distant from real life human decision making. Ostrom did not reject formalism or the use of mathematics, however she argued that we need to look at such models with great care. Often in economics, models that appear convincing are based on assumptions that can be challenged. Ostrom noted that the prisoner's dilemma and Olson's theory of collective action were closely related to the tragedy of the commons. All three models suggested logically that human cooperation to solve collective problems such as commons management was unlikely. Her approach was to view the tragedy as a potential problem and to take the formal model seriously. This reflects one of Ostrom's potential rules for radicals, which is to view issues of concern as problems and to engage in problem solving strategies where possible. Far from being tragic, Elinor believed that human beings could, if they understood such models, change their behaviour. Hardin's Malthusianism demands an authoritarian ecological politics, whereas Ostrom promotes a radically democratic approach to environmental problems.

It is worth looking briefly at the prisoner's dilemma and Olson's theory of action to see how they back up, in a more rigorous form, Hardin's pessimistic analysis. The prisoner's dilemma is a model made famous by another winner of the Nobel for Economics, John Nash. Nash, who was immortalised in the Hollywood film *A Beautiful Mind*, was a mathematical genius but suffered from severe mental health problems for much of his life. His Nash equilibrium has been used to suggest a likely outcome in the prisoner's dilemmas, which mitigates against cooperation and is consistent with Hardin's bleak approach to the commons.

Nash won the Nobel prize in 1984, along with John Harsanyi and Reinhard Selten for contributions to game theory. Game theory, as described by John von Neumann and Oskar Morgenstern in their classic book *Theory of Games and Economic Behavior*, is a study of strategic interactions (Neumann and Morgenstern 1944). While there are many different game scenarios that can be used to explain different situations, the prisoner's dilemma is probably the most famous.

If the prisoners cooperate with each other by refusing to confess to the policy they will both gain, escaping conviction because of lack of evidence. Such cooperation, according to Nash, was unlikely. Economists assume, generally, that we humans are rational maximisers, this means we try to maximise our own selfish interests. Both prisoners will assume that the other is a rational maximiser. If the prisoners both kept quiet, they would gain their freedom, however they assume that the other is likely to betray them. There is an incentive to be the first to confess because the first to confess would enjoy a reduced sentence. So, the likely Nash equilibrium will be that both will confess. Thus the pursuit of rational self-interest leads to what economists would term a sub-optimal solution. Both prisoners confess, so both go to jail. This logic applies equally to the commons; if different commoners cooperate, the collective gain from not ruining the commons will be large. Each commoner assumes that other commoners will be rationally self-interested so this leads to the assumption by any individual that if they conserve the commons, others will use it just as much or more and it will be ruined. This is spelt out in the passage from Hardin described earlier.

Ostrom noted that Olson's model of collective action, perhaps it should have been termed 'collective inaction', is another model which predicts that the commons will be ruined. Olson (1965) examined political and social movements and was critical of the idea that support for a particular ideology or set of policy demands was sufficient to persuade individuals to become politically active in a group. This was, again, essentially because of a free rider problem. Becoming politically engaged, joining a group, going on protest marches or helping with elections, are activities that demand a sacrifice of time and are costly in other ways. Each individual's contribution is so tiny that they might as well stay inactive and rely on the contribution of others. If everyone is rational this means that social and political movements will never take place because any individual will be inactive and attempt to free ride on the activism of others. The others, of course, will wait because they don't want to engage in time consuming activism either. In a commons context, no individuals will take positive action because others will take advantage of them doing so.

Social and political movements do occur, commons are not always tragic and, maybe, prisoners might cooperate, but all three formal models have a logic that seems to make sense. They suggest that human beings may find it difficult or even impossible to cooperate, leading to potentially catastrophic results. Elinor Ostrom was intrigued that while the formal models suggested that cooperation to conserve the commons was virtually impossible, her PhD work and Vince's research indicated that commons could be made to work. What was true in practice, she often argued, might be true in theory.

At the heart of each of these models is the free rider problem. Whenever one person cannot be excluded from the benefits that others provide, each person is motivated not to contribute to the joint effort and to 'free ride' on the efforts of others. If all participants choose to free-ride, the collective benefit will not be produced. The temptation to free-ride, however, may dominate the decision process, and thus all will end up where no one wanted to be. Alternatively, some may provide while others free-ride, leading to less than the optimal level of provision of the collective benefit. These models are thus extremely useful for explaining how perfectly rational individuals can produce, under some circumstances, outcomes that are not 'rational' when viewed from the perspectives of all those involved. (Ostrom 1990: 6)

Ostrom challenged the pessimistic conclusions of the formal models using the work of Robert Axelrod whose research suggested that trust could be created by what he termed strategies of tit for tat. Axelrod was politically active, especially around campaigns for peace, but like Elinor Ostrom he was interested in posing political dilemmas, such as the promotion of non-violence as practical problems. In his book *The Evolution of Cooperation* he argued that cooperative behaviour was selected for in the human species because it led to better outcomes than purely competitive behaviour. Of course, such an assumption might be seen as problematic; there is a long history of political thinkers arguing that aspects of biology including evolution can be used to prove particular perspectives on human society. The danger is that what we believe, we consciously or unconsciously project on to 'nature', and we then use nature to back up what we believe. There is a tradition of social Darwinism with supposed competition between species being used to justify capitalism, racism, imperialism, etc. Equally the efforts of those like Kropotkin who studied nature to suggest that cooperation was more likely might be criticised (1972). Axelrod's assumptions about evolution make sense but on their own they are inadequate. Incidentally the same might be said of formal models, they look logically convincing but their assumptions may be based on what we assume rather than on social reality.

Axelrod went further, backing up his analysis of the evolution of cooperation with a range of examples. He argued that 'tit for tat' strategies could be used to overcome the prisoner's dilemma. If we give something to the other person in the game, they may reciprocate, and the potential negative outcome may be overcome. Because cooperation leads to better outcomes than competition, there is a tendency for the cooperative outcomes to become more common. Of course, this might lead to a new reason for ignoring the problem of the commons. Whereas Hardin claimed that commons were always tragic, to suggest in contrast that commoners will always cooperate to conserve, is also problematic. While there is evidence for such cooperation, Ostrom did feel that there was potentially a real problem of conserving the commons, so it was important to look at how this could be done. Behind her design rules and extensive analysis, a key issue was trust.

Ostrom's analysis suggested that particular practices could be used to build trust. She found, for example, that research suggested that cheap talk was useful. By cheap talk, she meant that if commoners or others were able to communicate directly with each other, trust was more likely to occur than if they did not meet and exchange views. Her principles of commons design can be seen as ways to help to generate trust. Thus graduated sanctions work better than severe punishment because breaking commons rules may be a result of ignorance rather than selfishness. Pointing out a mistake or providing a minor sanction builds trust, where severe penalties will reduce trust. A word she used was 'scaffolding'. Rules and practices act to encourage some forms of behaviour and to discourage others; they work as a support or scaffold (Ostrom 1998). This assumption that individuals are supported in particular ways by particular forms of institutional scaffolding incidentally cuts through intellectual debates around free will and structuralism. Of course, we don't have complete free will but if we learn more about the structures that shape our behaviour we can gain more freedom.

Elinor Ostrom also argued that trust was essential to create democratic political systems. Only active participation of citizens based on an education for self-governance would sustain a democratic system. She wrote:

> For those who wish the twenty-first century to be one of peace, we need to translate our research findings on collective action into materials written for high school and undergraduate students. All too many of our textbooks focus exclusively on leaders and, worse, only national-level leaders. Students completing an introductory course on American government, or political science more generally, will not learn that they play an essential role in sustaining democracy. Citizen participation is presented as contacting leaders, organizing interest groups and parties, and voting. That citizens need additional skills and knowledge to resolve the social dilemmas they face is left unaddressed. (Ostrom 1998: 18)

Academic research can enhance human cooperation. Ostrom argued that we need to revolutionise our approach both to academic research and to education. Her work on education, science and democratic methods of learning is another area where I feel she was both instructive and radical. Chapter eight examines her approach to thinking and learning, moving beyond traditional academic methods, institutions and practices.

8

Science for the People

The tensions inherent in the work of the scientific community are, however, exceptionally high because belief is potentially contestable. Inquiry in the scientific tradition represents, then, a challenge to every form of orthodoxy. Further, there is a danger that scientific investigators may abandon modesty, presume to know the Truth, and create their own form of orthodoxy, while engaging in sweeping rejections of other forms of belief and failing to pursue the merit of the arguments that may be at issue. Dogmas advanced in the name of science are no less dogmatic than other dogmas. Efforts to destroy or silence others is a manifestation of dominance strategies that are repugnant to polycentricty in scientific communities.

(Ostrom in Ostrom and Ostrom 2014: 52)

Elinor Ostrom was interested in how academic work could empower citizens, how education could be made democratic and how intellectual endeavour could be shaped by grassroots participation. She believed that academic work was driven too much by intellectual elites and the insights of participants were often ignored. She felt that the research methodology, particularly in economics, was often simplistic. She also felt that a pluralist approach was important; she often cited what she described as the rule of the hammer. Social scientists were like carpenters obsessed with one tool, a hammer might be good for knocking in nails but was less effective at sawing through a piece of wood. Formal models and statistics might be useful in helping to understand some parts of social reality but historical case studies or even conversations with participants might be more effective in other circumstances. She tried to take a scientific approach to research but, above all, wanted to use intellectual work and education to promote self-organisation.

A number of philosophers, political thinkers and others have tried to think about how academic work and education can liberate individuals and social groups. For example, the Brazilian educational-ist Paulo Freire, who wrote the *The Pedagogy of the Oppressed*, argued that education was often elitist. He saw much education as being based on a banking model (Freire 1968). The teacher has knowledge, with which he or she fills the student. The student is passive and gathers information like a bank account or a jug being filled with water. In contrast education for liberation involves an interaction between teacher and student where both learn.

Freire, unlike Ostrom, was a Marxist but there are similarities in their approach. He starts with a teaching situation, she starts with a research project, but both believe in the co-production of knowledge rather than a top-down model. This challenges the essentialist notion of the teacher or researcher who is contrasted with a passive multitude with nothing to contribute to the process except their obedience. Teachers and students, researchers and participants are not eternally distinct and separate groups. Education for both thinkers is a two-way process, teachers and researchers need to listen as well as to speak.

Ostrom applied her ideas about knowledge creation mainly to research into the commons, however she also had ideas about teaching and learning which were very similar to Freire's.

Ostrom's broad approach, as we have seen, was to take a problem-based perspective and to use academic work to attempt to solve a particular, specific dilemma or puzzle. Her main specific problem was how to promote cooperative behaviour to conserve the commons. Her approach to this was to suggest that the people who participate in a commons are just as likely, probably more so, to have good ideas about solving this problem than outside experts. Garrett Hardin argued that the commoners would fail to maintain the commons and an outside power would need to be brought in. The outside power would be equipped with expertise that the commoners lack. This is a straightforward elitist view of knowledge production and the use of knowledge in society. Ordinary people who are not academics lack knowledge, academics make up an intellectual elite and government officials can use the expertise of academics to implement solutions. There are, of course, some sound arguments for this line of thought;

most of us would defer to the knowledge of doctors when we are ill or the expertise of engineers if we wanted to build a bridge.

Ostrom argued that intellectual work by academics was important but insufficient, that academics rarely have complete or adequate knowledge, and for both ethical and intellectual reasons participants should input into the knowledge process too. While academics may have studied a problem in detail and built up knowledge, participants are also likely to have knowledge and may understand factors that are invisible to outside experts. Also, irrespective of contributions to knowledge, Ostrom believed that outside experts had no right to dictate to communities and individuals. Solutions need to reflect what local communities want rather than what central authorities think is good for them. Ostrom was a strong believer in co-production, merging production and consumption, so that those of us gaining the final product whether it is health care, cans of beans or a working commons, can help shape what we receive (Ostrom 1996).

Economics as a discipline is often criticised for failing to take account of gender, social class and other social divisions that involved differential power. Economics seems a long way from co-production, its arcane jargon and often somewhat counter intuitive assumptions, make it inaccessible to most of us. Likewise, economics seems to ignore culture and other factors that cannot easily be quantified. So it might be thought that Elinor Ostrom would have rejected the reliance economists have on formal models and mathematical techniques. Given her battles as a woman to take an economics PhD because she was not taught enough mathematics at school, this might be thought to be the case too. In fact, Elinor Ostrom never rejected the methods of mainstream economics but felt that they had to be supplemented. She used statistical data and, as we have seen, was fascinated by formal models such as the prisoner's dilemma but felt other approaches were useful too. We return to her rule of the hammer; she might not think that a hammer was a good tool for all jobs but she didn't encourage us to throw away our hammers either. Formal models and econometrics had their role, but she liked multiple methods. She is sometimes criticised for being overly complex but she cannot be criticised for over reliance on one method to the exclusion of all others.

It is worth noting the distinction between methodology and method. A methodology is a broad approach to investigating social reality based on particular philosophical assumptions. A method is a precise technique used in actual research. Positivism and post-modernism can be described as methodologies. Postmodernism is sceptical of measurement and truth claims and argues that language shapes and mystifies any investigation into social reality. Positivism argues that only things that can be measured with precision can be investigated. Methods in social sciences like anthropology and sociology might include statistical surveys, interviews with participants, historical case studies or participant observation where researchers take part in the events they are studying. Economists tend to focus, almost exclusively, on statistical methods commonly known as econometrics.

Particular methods are often linked to particular methodologies. Economists are often seen as positivists but their methodology also makes use of formal logical models. Hardin's use of a formal model, essentially the prisoner's dilemma, that proved to be simplistic might be seen as a reason for rejecting formal models more generally. Although Hardin was a biologist his inspiration for formalism came from economics. Economics, at present, might be conceived as a vast network of interacting formal models. Marx too might be seen as presenting an alternative to mainstream economics also based on formal models. In turn, statistical investigation, known in economics as econometrics, is used to produce evidence to test the formal models. While formal models are often frowned upon and virtually all radicals are deeply suspicious of mainstream economics, there are some sound arguments for defending formalism.

Formalism uses deduction to build a logical argument which might be presented as a diagram or in algebraic form. The prisoner's dilemma is a classic example. It doesn't use evidence but instead produces a rigorous line of reasoning to support a suggested conclusion. We might criticise Hardin for failing to research actual commons but his use of the prisoner's dilemma did not need to rely on such investigations. A logical structure is constructed and particular conclusions are drawn. Very varied thinkers have advocated a formalist methodology. The Dutch philosopher Spinoza, free-market economist Ludwig von Mises, Karl Marx and the Marxist philosopher Althusser, all advocated formalism to some extent. This is because surface appearances may mislead us and may tell us little about the actual processes or causes of a phenomenon. In short, the evidence of our eye is no evidence. For example, to give a trivial but clear illustration, if we place a stick half submerged in water it looks as if it is bent but, of course, this is an illusion. Our senses are not precise scientific instruments. Marx argued that if essences and appearances coincided there would be no need for science (Parekh 2015: 54). He meant that if we could see atoms and molecules we would need little or no chemistry, the essence of how chemistry worked would be immediately visible.

There is also the sometimes misleading effect of common sense. We may be prisoners of deeply-held but erroneous views. There is always a danger that we select evidence unconsciously to back up views that we hold. A formal model based on logical argument wins, to repeat, for three reasons. First, it can be used to avoid unconscious biases by substituting inference based on appearance for logical chains of thought. Second, it can be used to understand underlying structures, whether in social or natural science, that cannot be easily observed. Third, even if there was no ideological bias, empirical evidence may be limited by our senses and even technological devices may not give a pure view. Marx, in writing *Capital*, was trying to build up a logical model of an economic system and to understand how it might evolve. Hardin's and others' uses of formal models at least show why human cooperation might be difficult to achieve. Von Mises also used logical models to understand economics. It is incidentally fascinating that thinkers with very different positions on the political spectrum held similar ideas about research methodology and method.

Yet, while there is much sense in the arguments in defence of formal models, their exponents can promote an elitist and top-down view of knowledge creation. Ostrom, to repeat, didn't reject formal models and was clear that if their assumptions were correct they would provide defensible conclusions. Nor was she a naive empiricist who believed that what ordinary people observed was always correct and the analysis of experts built on formal models was always incorrect. She certainly felt that formal models could be useful in framing questions and providing solutions. Her problem with using them to the exclusion of empirical methods based on popular participation, seems to have been based on a number of concerns. While I have not seen her frame it in this way, formalism is not immune from ideological assumptions. The way we construct a logical model depends on a number of assumptions and these assumptions may be shaped by pre-existing and perhaps false beliefs. The prisoner's dilemma is assumed to produce a sub-optimum result, where competitive behaviour leads to a loss of wellbeing compared to cooperative behaviour. However, while economists believe we are rational maximizers, Ostrom and other researchers have suggested that this is a doubtful assumption. Or, to be precise, while we might generally promote our own personal gain, we can also be cooperative, lack the information to be perfect individual maximizers and can potentially negotiate and communicate with others, to gain better results.

Formal models need to be tested with evidence, to see if key assumptions are true. Neither formal models nor empirical observation are perfect, using both is likely to be better than dependence on just one. Ostrom stressed complexity; in both human society and the rest of nature, multiple factors are likely to be important; a formal model may not capture all of these and the observations of participants may give some clues as to which factors are worthy of investigation.

Economics is empirical as well as formal. Formal models like demand and supply, comparative advantage (which suggests trade and exchange is efficient), etc. are supplemented with detailed statistical investigation known as econometrics. Economics is criticised for 'physics envy' and while in the past figures such as Adam Smith, Karl Marx, John Maynard Keynes and Hayek wrote books that were, at least, partially accessible to non-economists, economics is generally inaccessible to those of us without a degree in either economics or mathematics. Again, it might be thought that Ostrom was hostile to the mathematical turn in economics. Those of us on a vast spectrum from Marx to Hayek might celebrate her as a maths sceptic but this would be misleading; she thought mathematical approaches are useful but insufficient.

Like formalism, there are some persuasive arguments for econometrics. While we can't measure everything, this is not an argument for claiming we should measure nothing. We can also agree with the economist Deidre McCloskey (1985) that mathematics is shaped by assumptions that are cultural, so pure mathematics is limited by the kind of data we are seeking to describe. Economies, in turn, are highly complex, so can't be measured in all or even many significant respects. Nonetheless measurement in the form of econometrics is useful and important. A good example is the use of consequentialist arguments such as moral hazard to challenge the left. Consequentialists argue that state intervention to deal with inequality often leads to unforeseen consequences, which means leaving things to the market would be better. To challenge such consequentialism, often based on formal arguments, precise evidence is needed. The prisoner's dilemma can be seen as a consequentialist argument; enclosing and controlling the commons is essential because human kindness is a weak force that fails to guarantee conservation.

Free-market economists opposed to government intervention often use consequentialist arguments. One is moral hazard. If there is a problem in society that a government seeks to deal with, this may encourage individuals to be complacent, so on balance the problem may not be solved or it may be made worse. The 2008 financial crisis is widely perceived to be a result, partly at least, of moral hazard. Banks indulged in risky but potentially profitable practices because they knew that if this went wrong the government would bail them out. If we are in trouble and we know that the government will help us this form of moral hazard encourages us to take risks. The banks in countries like the UK were so large that if their risky practices led to bankruptcy this would in turn wreck the UK economy, so the government rescued them. We could examine this in terms of the growth of monopoly capitalism and invoke Marx and Lenin, but the point I am attempting to make is about the value of quantitative method. The positive effects of government intervention need to be balanced by any potential negative consequences. Unless we make some kind of numerical estimate it is impossible to assess the correct course of action.

A good example suggested by Peter Boettke, who is both a fine Ostrom scholar and a very free-market thinker, is the use of seat belts. Boettke has suggested that the introduction of seat belts, rather than saving lives, increased death rates because moral hazard encouraged drivers to drive more recklessly because they felt safer (Boettke 2012). While there are many variables and statistics are always limited, some use of quantitative methods might allow us to assess whether the positive effect of compulsory seat belts outweighed the negative. I suspect many of us would find the moral hazard argument quite weak in this context but evidence is vital; all of us risking being consciously or unconsciously biased. Quantitative techniques may contribute to reducing bias. Mathematics in the form of econometrics is clearly useful but is of course limited. Mathematics is circumscribed by both by the quality of the formal models used and the data gathered. Ostrom was not an opponent of quantitative method but rather an advocate of multiple methods of research.

Ostrom might be criticised for moving to the opposite extreme. Sometimes it appears as if she used every single method of social science research known to humanity and then added others from natural sciences in addition. She even used satellite data in several projects, because they provided evidence of tree cover that could be used to assess the effectiveness of different conservation strategies. I think on the whole her approach is extremely healthy and, as noted, different methods will work to solve or better understand particular problems. Formal models and econometrics are both useful but critically depend upon the soundness of the data collected and the assumptions used. Empirical evidence on its own may be flawed and subject to vast misunderstanding, but it can allow us to see whether formal models are built on sound assumptions. Statistics tend to generate correlations but these could just be coincidences; both formal methods and further empirical investigation may help us to move beyond correlations to investigate possible causes.

Ostrom's approach is similar in some ways to the Austrian-born philosopher of science, Paul Feyerabend, who wrote *Against Method*. Feyerabend, who claimed to be an anarchist methodologist and freely quotes both Brecht and Hayek, argues that no one methodological school produces adequate knowledge (Feyerabend 1975). He stressed multiple methodologies and methods and noted the role of accident in knowledge production. While it is an exaggeration to say that he was actually against method or felt that anything goes in research, he argued that different methodology often led to useful knowledge. Attempts to prove that one methodology is The Methodology and others are inferior are unlikely to succeed. Accidents and irrationality play their party. He notes with some satisfaction that the pursuit of Renaissance Hermetic Magic helped lead, via a chain of consequences, to Galileo's valuable work in science. Progress is not always a narrative of smooth accumulation as science overcomes superstition. While Ostrom did not go as far as Feyerabend's anarchist approach to knowledge creation her sympathies link her to his writings.

Both Elinor and Vincent were critical of the notion that researchers could be entirely neutral. This assumption which is held by positivists argues that researchers should try to rid themselves of any subjective viewpoint to produce scientific conclusions. The Ostroms argued that social sciences could not be treated in a totally objective manner. The opinions of participants powerfully shaped situations. Beliefs, even if false, had a material effect. For example, if one believes in the truth of the 'tragedy of the commons', that will influence how you treat a commons. Government officials persuaded by Hardin's viewpoint will promote 'enclosure'. This insight makes research and policy making difficult, we can never totally separate belief, true or false, from more measurable and stable factors. Researchers have viewpoints and perhaps can never be objective. This is another reason why the Ostrom support for multiple methods is useful. As a school student she was a member of the debating society and having argued on one side of an argument, would be required to argue the opposing point of view (Ostrom 2010b: 2). This is a healthier approach perhaps than promoting a neutrality that might be unrealistic in practice.

This challenge to totally objective research standpoints chimes with Austrian economics, which is a free-market school of thought, and also a range of forms of radical social science. The challenge is to be sceptical of essentialism, positivism and neutrality, while still undertaking research that provides practical conclusions. This is a big ask but better than assuming rather simplistic notions about how research can generate relevant conclusions.

Elinor Ostrom also believed in a team approach to research. She believed that if multiple methods were vital and that both social and natural sciences were important in investigating the commons and other problems of sustainability, no one individual was likely to be able to complete research alone. She often participated on projects with other researchers, co-wrote much of her work and suggested that her work could not be separated from that of Vincent Ostrom or other members of their workshop. Ultimately the commoners or other participants are part of the research team, the divide between academics and the rest of humanity is strongly eroded in her approach to research.

Academics increasingly seem to pursue a logic of individualistic competitiveness. Big name researchers command high salaries. The quest for knowledge seems to be substituted by the promotion of individuals. Money, too, increasingly talks. Academic work is quantified and used to promote funding. Research seems to be yet another product of individualism and market values. Ostrom stated her support for methodological individualism but if we look at the fruits of her academic labour they tend to be highly based on team work and a collective approach. The notion of private property seems to have entered research, with individuals owning knowledge. Implicit in Ostrom's work is the notion that knowledge is always to some extent co-produced.

She also sought to cumulate knowledge. She and Vincent argued that much intellectual labour especially in political science was about defending one school of thought from another. Too often they felt that there was little emphasis on trying to accumulate knowledge and gain greater understanding. Both Ostroms were keen on what they termed 'contestation', by which they meant no holds barred argument and critical debate, but this was combined with an opposition to what might be described as academic sectarianism. While the Ostroms had some strong underlying assumptions such as a concern with deep democracy, scepticism of the state, diversity and ecological sustainability, they tended to be problem orientated. This meant that academic work was less about the defence of a particular viewpoint and more an emphasis on problem solving. Ostrom did not advocate collective ownership as a universal solution but instead focused on solving the problem of how cooperation, where necessary, could be promoted. If research suggested that some of her ideas were wrong, she tended to change her ideas. Typically, she revised her eight design rules for a successful commons in the light of research by others in the field.

The accumulation of knowledge, from this perspective, is always limited because of Ostrom's anti-essentialism and pluralism, one solution or one form of analysis is unlikely to fit all situations. There are no, or at least few, truths that are relevant for ever and in all circumstances. Nonetheless she sought to see how previous research could be built upon. To do so require creating where possible a common language. She noted the existence of a tower of Babel problem because different disciplines used different terminologies, so comparing findings was difficult. One of her key tasks in researching the commons was to find ways of comparing the research undertaken by different researchers in different fields.

Ostrom's method might be criticised for its methodological individualism. This is the assumption held by liberal political philosophers and most economists that we are rational, largely self-sufficient individuals with free will who can make clear choices. Many thinkers on the left have dismissed such individualism as unrealistic; we are shaped by society and culture. Spinoza challenged individualism, arguing that we are the product of causes we don't control. To some extent Ostrom came to see such methodological individualism as intellectually insufficient and noted that investigation into social structures is important (Ostrom 2004). However, built into both her and Vincent's work from the earliest days is the assumption that if individuals have greater understanding of social forces we can make more informed choices.

Debates around individual freedom versus determinism run through social science and practical politics but while often stressing individual freedom the Ostroms argued that politics was a craft similar in some ways to a physical pursuit such as sculpture or carpentry. If we know our materials, we can use them better. Vincent Ostrom in his 1980 paper 'Artisanship and Artifact' explored this concept in some depth. The Ostroms made their own furniture and saw a physical productive craft as fundamentally similar to academic labour. Gravity and other natural forces cannot be suspended by human agency but we can work with them for better results. This is a useful compromise on the structuralism debate, we can be freer if we understand forces, qualities and structures better. Thus participants co-produce knowledge with academics, participants have access to information so called experts may lack, but academics can cumulate both the knowledge of previous academic investigations and participants. This may make it easier to tackle particular problems but may not provide conclusions which are universally applicable.

In turn, Elinor Ostrom argued that democracy was unlikely to be effective and commons were less likely to be conserved without participatory education. Political education was limited because it might explain constitutions, political parties and even ideologies but it did not show how individuals could participate in the construction of their own political structures. Politics in the form of governance runs through the whole of society. Making choices about maintaining the commons or agreeing how to share parking lots are just as much politics as the work of a parliament or executive body. So, as well as having radical thoughts about research Elinor Ostrom was also an education radical. Top-down didactic education was generally rejected and interactive participatory learning was promoted. Thus the Ostroms developed their research centre as the workshop, a place for participation rather than passive lecturing.

Implicit in all of this is a challenge to dominant elitist ideas of academic work and education. All of us participate in politics but political science is practiced by a tiny group of academics; in turn, the academics may promote individual careers rather than collective knowledge production. Schools of academic thought too often resemble religious sects, focused on boundary maintenance through criticism of other schools of thought. The Ostrom approach is to note that any material practice from cooking to carpentry involves design, such design is an intellectual task that has an effect. Design can be both collective and participatory. Academic work may separate intellectual work from effects and promote romantic ideas of uniquely creative individuals who make world changing discoveries. The Ostroms challenged these assumptions confronting academic individualism, romanticism and sectarianism. Rather charmingly,

Elinor dedicated *Governing the Commons* to Vincent for his 'love and contestation'.

Elinor Ostrom, while rejecting commons as a universal solution, did seem to see research as a commons. She was particularly keen to promote knowledge sharing and was critical of intellectual copyright that prevented individuals and research teams from building on the findings of previous academic work. As such she investigated, most notably in a book co-written with Charlotte Hess, the ideas of a knowledge commons (Hess and Ostrom 2011).

The assumption that ideas are produced by individuals who can then trade them is inconsistent with Ostrom's approach. The idea of a knowledge commons helps accelerate research into difficult problems like human cooperation or dealing with climate change. There is a battle to keep knowledge enclosed and tradeable. The Ostroms established an international library of free-to-use articles on commons and related topics. Again, the paradox is that while she was often conceptualised as a liberal and she generally believed in methodological individualism, she was a strong advocate of the collective production of knowledge.

Her work stressed physical commons in land and seas and much of it was carried out before the creation of the World Wide Web, yet her investigations seem relevant to the uses of knowledge promoted in cyber space. Concepts of open source and free software fit very well indeed with an Ostrom approach.

The Ostrom approach to research and education was put into practice at the workshop. Here students and academic staff would work on projects. The title 'workshop' seems to fit with the ideas of academic work being a craft, so you can have a workshop to make furniture, or a workshop to make items on three dimensional printers or to produce academic knowledge. One former workshopper I asked about this said that the title was convenient because the university authorities did not understand what it meant, and because of this left the Ostroms to their own devices! The Ostrom workshop did nonetheless seem to cause minor scandal and some disquiet to other university staff. One participant remembered:

My first memory of a Workshop event occurred before the event, its purpose now long forgotten. I was walking across the Bloomington campus with a member of the political science faculty when he turned to me and offered advice to the effect of, be careful about getting involved over there or you may find yourself counting trees in Nepal. (Fotos 2013: 8)

The workshop was established in 1973 as the Workshop in Political Theory and Policy Analysis and renamed after the deaths of Elinor and Vincent in 2012 in their honour. 'The term "workshop" represents the conviction that the skills for this type of research are best acquired and used in a setting where students, working as apprentices and journeymen, have the opportunity to collaborate with experienced scholars' (https://ostromworkshop.indiana.edu/about/history/index. html). Multiple methods and strong contestation were encouraged. Typically, Elinor Ostrom took an early draft of her Nobel speech to the workshop and encouraged workshoppers to criticise it, so that she could rewrite it.

She did not feel that perfect knowledge was possible or that academics always knew best. She argued that participation was both democratic and through collective effort could effectively crowd source potential solutions to problems. This reflects the peer to peer technique that has emerged with the creation of the World Wide Web. She wrote:

The intellectual trap in relying entirely on models to provide the foundation for policy analysis is that scholars that presume that they are omniscient observers able to comprehend the essentials of how complex, dynamic systems work by creating stylized descriptions of some aspects of those systems. With the false confidence of presumed omniscience, scholars feel perfectly comfortable in addressing proposals to governments that are conceived in their models as omnicompetent powers able to rectify the imperfections that exist in all field settings. (Ostrom 1990: 215)

In short, the intellectual trap occurs because academics are over confident in their models and assumptions. Science needs an injection of doubt and findings need to be seen in a context.

In summary, she was an educational and intellectual radical committed to democratic participation. She rejected the romantic idea of an individual author or intellectual who could make discoveries independently of others because of their unique insight. She instead saw research as a collective project. She rejected too the idea of sectarian intellectual schools. She focused upon problem solving rather than the defence of a particular viewpoint. Radical demands for cooperation, deep democracy, participation and diversity are possible, because essentialist arguments around human nature cannot be used to shut them down. Detailed investigation of what works and what doesn't work can be used by we fallible but creative and capable humans to try to achieve such goals. Research uses knowledge cumulated in the past, utilises diverse research methods and comes up with broad, helpful solutions to practical problems, Ostrom, of course, mainly focused on the problem of sustainability. We could argue that if an alternative to neoliberalism is desired, part of the solution is to investigate alternatives, to see what has worked and what has failed. Structural influences need to be taken into account; in a capitalist society cooperatives may fail because they have to compete and prioritise short term profit instead of community values. However, case studies of cooperatives or other forms of workers' control could be used to construct broad design rules for collective economics institutions. The politics of perhaps revolutionary social change is needed but we cannot wait for the revolution and insist things will automatically be better. Different institutions and practices will be needed and Ostrom points the way to understanding these better. Chapter nine examines her institutional perspectives in more detail.

9

Transforming Institutions

[N]o single form of organization is 'good' for all circumstances
and events. Any particular organizational or institutional form has
certain capabilities and is subject to specific sources of weakness
or failure. Given the problem of institutional weaknesses by
continuously adapting and adjusting the organizational patterns,
in function of shifting circumstances and preferences, is essential.

(Aligică and Sabetti 2014: 8)

When I interviewed Elinor Ostrom, a couple of months before her
death in 2012, she told me proudly that she was not an economist but
a political economist. More specifically, she was institutionalist and
noted on more than one occasion that what she and Vincent did was
to study institutions. Political parties are institutions and their rules
shape their internal politics. Economies can be seen as institutional,
with human beings making decisions which are influenced by organisations and practices.

A commons, as a legal structure of property ownership, is an
institution. Ostrom's commons work was very much about mapping
institutions. She examined commons that were well conserved to see
which rules seemed to promote good and sustainable use. Even if
formal concepts of property are rejected, commoners work within
rules and norms that shape how they interact with each other and
their environment. She described the rules she saw. More precisely
she set up a system for mapping institutions known as Institutional
Analysis and Development (IAD). Her IAD approach described
a particular framework of rules, examining how they might shape
strategic interactions from participating members. This seems a
rather obvious but important method. Elinor believed that an IAD
approach, by making it easier to understand an institution, might
make it easier to reform to make it work better. IAD analysis allows

us to understand a particular social institution. Institutions can be seen as games, understanding the rules precisely is a step towards winning the game. Elinor, of course, was interested in cooperative games, developing cooperative strategies, rather than promoting winners over losers.

There is much debate amongst institutional economists and others as to what is meant by an institution. Elinor Ostrom argued, 'Broadly defined, institutions are the prescriptions that humans use to organize all forms of repetitive and structured interactions including those within families, neighborhoods, markets, firms, sports leagues, churches, private associations, and governments at all scales' (Ostrom 2005: 3). She has also observed that institutions were marked by 'shared concepts used by humans in repetitive situations organized by rules, norms, and strategies' (Ostrom 2010c: 263).

By rules she meant 'prescriptions (must, must not, or may) that are mutually understood and predictably enforced in particular settings', these are enforced by agents who can monitor and punish if they are broken. Ostrom 2010c: 263). In economics, rules include forms of legal regulation that firms must abide by; minimum wage is an example of a rule. However, rules don't have to be decided and enforced by the state, an organisation, say a church will have rules, while games such as chess are structured by rules.

For her, norms were more informal, essentially self-reinforced rules, seen as allowing or preventing particular choices of behaviour. Strategies for her were 'regularized plans that individuals might make' (Ostrom 2010c: 263). Norms can perhaps be seen as habits, elements of culture that we learn and, once learnt, shape our reactions.

Strategies, in turn, are methods that individuals might use within an institution to attempt to achieve particular goals. The 'tit for tat' strategy, for example, sees individuals rewarding others who cooperate with them. When firms compete through a price war this is another strategy. As the game of chess indicates, there may be an almost infinite number of strategies that might be used by individuals in an attempt to win the game.

She suggested that describing institutions made up of such formal rules and more informal norms was difficult because they were often invisible. 'Because institutions are fundamentally invisible, shared concepts that exist in the minds and routines of participants in policy situations, we believe policy analysis must include a careful survey of how participants actually do things and why they do them one way rather than another' (Polski and Ostrom 1999: 3).

Rules in form are less important than the rules in use. Rules in use may actually contradict the written formal laws, which can make institutional research very challenging. 'The dos and don'ts that one learns on the ground that may not exist in any written document. In some instances, they may actually be contrary to the dos and don'ts that are written in formal documents' (Ostrom 2010c: 263).

To understand institutions, she was convinced that we had to look at them in detail rather than using broad terms like capitalism, liberal democracy or fascism to provide guides. Often in politics we are fixed on broad slogans that suggest powerful structures act to create social and economic reality. Her approach was to look at how actual institutions work in practice. A good illustration of her work might be achieved by viewing the well-known US TV series *The Wire* (2002–08), which looks at how fictional Baltimore police do battle with local drug dealers. It rather persuasively illustrates a number of Elinor Ostrom's themes about institutions, society and politics. For a start, big interventionist government policies like 'the war on drugs', or attempts to promote educational achievement using standardised tests, can go horribly wrong. It is also pleasingly morally ambiguous; this isn't just about good guys and bad. The central character McNulty is a very flawed police officer, and the details of how surveillance is used and misused in *The Wire* are interesting and instructive. Above all, it is about institutions and how in practice they can be understood. There are formal rules but these are often ignored, individuals are often in competition, including some good illustrations of local politicians battling it out. The global trends and economic forces do have an influence in *The Wire*, for example, much of series two is shaped by neoliberalism's effect on traditional working-class jobs in the docks. The once powerful dock union loses power because containerisation means that far fewer workers are needed and jobs disappear. Containerisation can be seen as a strategy to weaken powerful unions and drive profits up. Yet the big capitalist story is not the only one that drives the plot. Accidents, competition, cooperation, personal rivalries and changes in rules that lead to unforeseen consequences are all apparent. If you think institutions are boring or irrelevant, watch *The Wire* and think again.

INSTITUTIONAL ANALYSIS AND DEVELOPMENT

Ostrom's institutional mapping was literal. She produced diagrams showing institutions. The basic IAD model was used by her, for example, to describe social-ecological systems. Michael McGinnis (2011) from the Ostrom workshop has provided a step by step guide to constructing an institutional map. He defines institutions in terms of their effects, cutting through the various arguments about their exact nature, to observe 'Institutions are human-constructed constraints or opportunities within which individual choices take place and which shape the consequences of their choices' (McGinnis 2011: 170). Analysis is also rather crisply defined by him as the 'decomposition of institutional contexts into their component parts as a prelude to understanding how these parts affect each other and how institutions shape outcomes' (McGinnis 2011: 170). By breaking down or decomposing the parts of an institution, we can see how it works or fails to do so.

McGinnis further notes that in constructing an IAD to describe a particular institution, inputs, outputs and an action situation can be described. Inputs are seen as including 'all aspects of the social, cultural, institutional, and physical environment'. So, for a common pool resource they might include ecological factors, beliefs about conservation, and rules set up to conserve the commons. Obviously if the IAD is too detailed it will be confusing and unwieldy; what is the use of a map that is the same scale as the physical reality? Outputs are the consequences of the interaction of human beings and indeed other species within the institutional setting. For example, soil erosion versus a good harvest in a commons might be conceived as outputs. The action situation is the 'black box' where choices are made. He notes participants 'evaluate actions, outputs, and outcomes, and these evaluations may affect any stage of the process' (McGinnis 2011: 172).

There are different institutional levels, and constitution making can be seen as setting up the rules that create an institution. There may be rules, in turn, to determine how the rules are made. If we understand different institutional levels, we are better placed to change them. This institutional language is often lost in politics. We debate what we would like politicians to do, we are not used to getting involved ourselves and helping to construct institutions. In Ostrom's deep democracy, participation in rule making becomes crucial. As she suggested, people are more likely to agree to rules they have made themselves. The construction of rules to decide how rules are made can be understood as constitution building. Constitutions are seen as grand political structures such as the US constitution but according to Elinor and other exponents of her IAD approach, can be found in many diverse areas of human life.

The action situation is the institutional setting within which we make decisions. A political leadership contest could, for example, be an action setting. A season in the water meadows of a Wiltshire commons might be another example. This isn't a context where Ostrom would assume us to be either working exclusively for our own selfish goals, or instead purely doing the common good. Our motives are likely to be mixed, and our knowledge too will be incomplete. By understanding the rules of the game we are better placed to win, but Ostrom stressed the creation of cooperation. Indeed, in a commons, if we can overcome the supposed tragedy we can collectively do better than if we stick with a selfish approach.

Ostrom used seven characteristics to describe an action situation. These included (1) the participants, for example, commoners, members of a political party, bank staff, etc., depending on the context. (2) Positions are the particular actions that participants can take, for example, putting more cattle on the commons or taking days off of work by throwing a sicky, or voting for a particular candidate in an election. (3) Outcomes are the results, for example, the election of a new party leader, or the loss of milk because of over-grazing, or a small bonus for staff. (4) Action-outcome linkages are the way in which the moves that participants make can be linked to the results. The prisoner's dilemma is used to show how actions such as confessing make both prisoners worse off compared to keeping quiet. (5) The control that the participants exercise is also a feature of Ostrom's analysis; formal power may be different to the control, weak or strong, that participants effectively have. (6) Information is another factor. Greater knowledge of an institutional setting helps participants to reshape the institutions. Finally, (7) particular costs and benefits might be assigned to the action taken, these in turn increase the likelihood of particular outcomes.

IADs are dynamic. A particular situation, say a general election or negotiation over commons use, will lead to institution change that shapes action situations in the future.

Ostrom's social-ecological systems approach is basically a form of IAD framework but natural sciences are used to enhance the model. The micro sociology of how humans behave given particular institutions is combined with ecological factors.

The IAD approach can seem abstract and over complex. It is also limited in that it has generally been used specifically to look at local commons and SES rather than practiced and refined in diverse contexts. It is also a new way of thinking about politics or, at least, an approach to political change and institutions with which we are perhaps unfamiliar. Exclusion from politics, other than occasional voting, is the norm. Active and perhaps continual participation is rather radical!

Marx wrote of how the manipulation of institutional rules was used to capture commons from the commoners:

Communal property – always distinct from the State property just dealt with – was an old Teutonic institution which lived on under cover of feudalism. We have seen how the forcible usurpation of this, generally accompanied by the turning of arable into pasture land, begins at the end of the 15th and extends into the 16th century. But, at that time, the process was carried on by means of individual acts of violence against which legislation, for a hundred and fifty years, fought in vain. The advance made by the 18th century shows itself in this, that the law itself becomes now the instrument of the theft of the people's land, although the large farmers make use of their little independent methods as well. The parliamentary form of the robbery is that of Acts for enclosures of

Commons, in other words, decrees by which the landlords grant themselves the people's land as private property, decrees of expropriation of the people. Sir F. M. Eden refutes his own crafty special pleading, in which he tries to represent communal property as the private property of the great landlords who have taken the place of the feudal lords, when he, himself, demands a 'general Act of Parliament for the enclosure of Commons' (admitting thereby that a parliamentary *coup d'état* is necessary for its transformation into private property), and moreover calls on the legislature for the indemnification for the expropriated poor. (Marx 1976: 885–886)

As Marx argued, institutional rules are written and rewritten to change power relationships. A good current example is the Transatlantic Trade and Investment Platform (TTIP), which is being negotiated between the North American Free Trade Area (NAFTA) and the European Union. This would standardise various rules around consumer and environmental welfare between member countries. Critics fear that the rules introduced would lead to reduced protection for workers, consumers and the environment. Opponents of TTIP also suggest that it would make it possible for firms to take legal action against governments if governments damaged firms' profit margins. Such a massive piece of institutional reframing would transform the power of governments and provide more power for corporations. TTIP and similar agreements have been well publicised but there are numerous pieces of international institutional architecture that may be invisible to most of us but shape our lives.

Too often power is seen in a conspiratorial and hidden way. An attention to institutions moves us from imagining all-powerful and sinister enemies, to an ability to potentially open institutions to democratic control. Radical politics might be defined by its approach to institutional rules; radical objectives demand that the rules are rewritten. Property rests on legal rules. Cooperative, collective and diverse alternatives will need different sets of legal relations. Property rights can be transformed in a more cooperative and ecological direction. Unforeseen consequences are always likely to occur, but different legal structures can help us create a different society. In turn, institutions are often invisible, we can't see the rules in action because they differ from what is written down. Yet while institutional analysis is not always easy, it provides a tool that can be used to explore institutional arrangements that may otherwise be forgotten.

At present, corporations generally have a legal requirement to maximise profits for shareholders. Rewriting legislation to promote the idea of ecological usufruct is an alternative. Usufruct, derived from Roman law, is the right to use property which is owned by others, as long as we leave it in just as good a condition as we found it. This suggests an institutional rule for promoting long-term sustainability rather than short-term self-interest. It is implicit in Elinor Ostrom's praise for the seven-generation rule. Radical movements need institutional analysis to defend and conserve, and they also need institutional analysis to help win political battles. Equally, institutional analysis can be used to shape better structures.

Institutional change is a vital tool for creating a more equal and ecological future. Both Ostrom and the radical authors Negri and Hardt see corporations as a form of legal commons. Marx modelled a capitalist economy based on individual entrepreneurs who competed with each other but he saw corporate governance as gradually replacing individual ownership. Implicit in Lenin's approach, and perhaps even Marx's, was that a capitalist economy, paradoxically, was innately collective. Corporations might be turned from shareholdings to truly collective property owned by society in general. Ostrom, in turn, was supportive of workers' cooperatives. If the aim of Marx was to promote a society based on a free association of workers, IAD analysis might help us think about economic structures that promote collective ownership which is economically, ecologically and socially beneficial.

However, Ostrom also reminds us that if we construct institutional blueprints, failure is likely. Institutional analysis is important and she believed that human beings often strive for better institutions. However, no one group is likely to have the 'answer', institutional development should occur constantly and engage citizens in general. A socialist committee that designs a socialist future is a long way from the Ostrom method. The purely free-market idea that institutional development is largely unnecessary since market forces work to promote efficiency can also be rejected. Vincent Ostrom argued that because no one model worked perfectly in all circumstances, communities need to keep adapting and reinventing institutions.

Elinor Ostrom sought alternatives beyond the market and the state, suggesting that markets, states and commons arrangements were just shorthand for describing some forms of institutions. She believed that, while we humans are imperfect and cannot design utopia, we can move beyond the institutions we are familiar with and build better futures.

Understanding how particular institutions work allows us to better challenge, change or conserve them. Ostrom's institutional analysis provides, I feel, a powerful tool for doing so. A map of reality makes it easier for us to change reality. Ostrom's work is essential to creating effective social change towards a more equal and ecological society, however she would have been the first to admit that her work was only a contribution; diversity is needed in our approaches if they are to be effective. Nonetheless if you can map flows of power, even in a crude way, you are in a better position to change the flows. Chapter ten concludes by looking at how Ostrom's work can be assessed as a means of promoting and sustaining positive social change.

Conflict and Contestation

It is less about the nature of power relations and the exercise of power, and more about problem solving and the ordering of things; less about command and obedience and more about balancing and coordination; less about Machiavellian statecraft, and more about citizens' competence; less about Hobbesian sovereignty, and more about Tocquevillian democracy.

(Castiglione 2014: xv)

This last chapter examines what we on the left can learn from Ostrom's work, provides some criticism and concludes with a summary of some practical implications of her approach. She did not promote collective ownership as a universal solution to all human ills nor did she work to overthrow capitalism. Nonetheless she did challenge the colonial, conservative and authoritarian assumptions that might be derived from the 'tragedy of the commons' perspective. Conservative politics might be seen as based on some notion of original sin, suggesting that human beings are inevitably greedy and flawed, so we need strong discipline to keep us under control. Ostrom shows that, while we are far from perfect, we can often cooperate. The authoritarianism of Hardin's views are closely linked to a colonial perspective that suggests that white western experts need to be in charge. There is a rather dubious and racist history of conservation involving representatives of European colonial powers removing land from local people because they are viewed as degrading it.

There are many examples from Africa; William Beinart, the environmental historian, notes that both colonial and many postcolonial governments viewed traditional forms of land ownership on the continent as destructive. But what he described as an 'avalanche of studies' in range ecology has challenged this view. The assumption that the Baringo in Kenya degraded land because of communal cattle grazing was not backed up by botanical evidence. Equally, the Tribal Grazing Land Policy introduced in Botswana in the 1970s, which semi-privatised previous communal grazing rights, led to greater inequality and environmental degradation (Beinart 2000). There are similar examples of enclosure and removal of commons from across the globe. Yet despite the work of Ostrom and other researchers like Beinart, commons are still being enclosed and destroyed. It is also important to note that economists or individuals from other disciplines might have logical arguments to defend the tragedy of the commons or other assumptions, but such arguments often prove in practice to be flawed. The consequences of accepting that commons are tragic and bound to fail continues to be damaging, with such arguments still used to steal land and impoverish people.

There are a number of other insights that radicals can take from Elinor Ostrom's writings and practical research. First, models and arguments suggested by economists and others that provide seemingly convincing arguments against cooperation, may sometimes simply be false or at least misleading. We need to investigate both the logic of the assumptions of such models and whether in practice they stand up; often they may not. Second, if cooperation is possible in the perhaps difficult task of maintaining commons, it is likely to be possible in other areas of society. So, while Ostrom was definitely not a communist, she provides inspiration for those on the left who think a more collective approach is worth promoting. Third, she urges us to take a pragmatic, problem solving approach and look in detail at how to make an institution work or how to try to deal with a particular issue. As radicals we may be tempted to look at politics and economics in abstract way, developing principles and defending beliefs but failing to intervene and have an effect in particular circumstances. Fourth, she suggests that a blueprint for the development of a utopian solution is unlikely to conserve or improve the commons. I think this might be applied more widely on the left; we can't come up with detailed universal solutions, we need to outline principles that generally work but be open to diversity.

Despite all these positive features, Ostrom's work can be challenged in a number of ways. It is possible to engage in a robust Marxist critique of Elinor Ostrom's work. I think she would have quite liked this. My intuition from having met her and enjoyed some obsessive study of her work is that criticism was welcomed. What she and Vincent often got was not criticism, but silence and dismissal. They were both often told that their research was without value and that they were asking questions that didn't matter. Criticism is better than silence. Contestation, the term they used for strong intellectual debate, was something they were rather enthusiastic about. Again, this fits with the emphasis on problem solving rather than taking an intellectual position and defending it against all comers. Elinor Ostrom's work was about pursuing particular questions rather than promoting an ideologically preconditioned set of answers that one fights for and challenges other approaches to. So I am going to examine how we can criticise her work particularly, but briefly, from a broadly Marxist point of view. I will in turn look at how Marx's approach to the commons and collective ownership might be criticised from an Ostrom perspective. It is then possible to look at what both Ostrom and Marx had in common and subject this to further debate. While there are a range of schools of radical political thought, clearly both Marx and Ostrom studied commons with care, so to my mind it is especially important to contrast them. All of this aims to refine our rules for radicals and promote some practical action. Theory is merely distraction unless linked to activity, it might be suggested.

I will try to be brief. I have already criticised aspects of Ostrom's work from a broadly Marxist perspective in some detail previously (Wall 2014a and b). Also, the criticism can rest on one simple, rather banal but equally brutal point. This is that the commons didn't fail because of a breakdown in trust and cooperation by the commoners but instead the commons were enclosed, stolen and shut down by capitalists, imperialists and various species of the rich and powerful. The whole debate around 'the tragedy of the commons' is perhaps irrelevant. The micro political economy of managing the commons could be seen as a distraction. The macro factors at the level of social class, historical change and states is what matters. Ostrom's work, some critics might argue, is thus not a form of analysis but a form of forgetting. Or to be more precise, she is so focused on the individual trees, she misses the forest. Marx didn't forget the forest, and we know this to be literally so. Engels argued that what turned Marx towards communism and his economic analysis in *Capital* was the criminalisation of peasants who asserted their common right to pick up fallen wood in the forest.

The point is that in a capitalist economic system communal property and collective rights are progressively and often violently eroded. Marx described this using the case study of England in Chapter 26 of *Capital* Volume 1. Engels did much the same for the German commons in *The Mark*, originally a supplement to *Socialism: Utopian and Scientific* (Engels 1928). The commons are something that we have to fight for, the tragedy is not misuse or failure which can be investigated by game theory, but the brutality of class warfare. The Ostrom problem is, to repeat, from a Marxist perspective, a non-problem.

In turn, questions of cooperation and trust are products of larger social forces rather than the more local interaction of individuals. The Ostroms' work was built on methodological individualism, we individuals are sovereign and free. More structural analysis suggest that this is a false assumption. The determinism of Spinoza is perhaps behind much Marxist analysis that says we are products of society and don't have freedom to choose. Spinoza, the seventeenth-century excommunicated Jewish thinker, argued that to be free we cannot be the product of causes external to us, but who can say this? We are all products of society, nature and culture. While Spinoza's determinism contradicts perhaps his own support for democracy and republicanism, he has a strong point. Human beings are shaped by other human beings. We can't justify intellectually the idea that individuals have freedom to shape their own futures, independent of social structures. Elements of our society such as language and indeed the Ostroms' beloved institutions are products of human action, but also shape and limit our action. Methodological individualism is basically false. It would be wrong to say human individuals have no freedom but the idea that we are autonomous is incorrect. We don't have sovereign power over our individual destinies. So the argument is that the macro factors are key and the micro largely derivative. Thus, crudely put, revolution is necessary to transform an entire social structure. Norms, rules and the rest are products of a social whole.

The obvious response from an Ostrom position is provided by Vincent Ostrom in a paper criticising Lenin. Vincent's approach was to read political thinkers closely before critiquing them. His method was to reconstruct their own arguments as clearly as possible and to present them in a broadly sympathetic way. Once this was achieved, criticism could begin. To some extent, Ostrom's critique was part of the contest of the Cold War, with pro- and anti-Soviet academics fighting their own intellectual cold war. However, Vincent was obviously supportive of the Marxist wish to bring about the 'withering away of the state'. Vincent's work combined a nod to right-wing free-market economists, along with a concern for sustainability and a radically democratic society. His critique of Lenin was that with revolution, a different society would need to be created, but without a close attention to institutions this was impossible. It is not enough to say the social transformation of revolution would give rise to the rules, norms and practices that would do away with the state and introduce a functioning communist society.

I am not sure that Elinor Ostrom was ever interested in discussing Lenin but her analysis is built on this point. Structural macro analysis is not the only or main analysis necessary. We can read a society purely from its macro sociological structures. A number of other levels of analysis are also in her view significant.

There is tentative evidence that both Marx and the Ostroms were aware of these types of criticisms and counter-criticism. I don't think Vincent built a time machine and badgered Karl about institutions, but Marx in his later writings became more and more interested in the indigenous and actual working commons. Instead of finishing his master work *Das Kapital*, he engaged in the study of anthropology.

Equally Elinor and Vince, I feel, were defending methodological individualism in a fairly nuanced way. They didn't see human beings as separate from structures or networks; after all, their work is about human cooperation and how this is influenced by institutional factors. Yet they argued that, that despite being dependent on others and being influenced by social factors, individuals have the ability to take choices and to make change.

While I am strongly critical of methodological individualism, because it is methodologically naive, I am aware that it was used by the Ostroms to argue for radical democracy. There is a danger that critics of methodological individualism see some people as determined and others as determiners. Elite democracy isn't working well at present, and even if it did, it is ethically and morally wrong. We need a democracy based on participation and this was at the heart of much of the Ostroms' concern and is vitally important.

Both Marx and Ostrom, if in some imagined, time-travel mediated conference call on commons, would agree on the necessity for broadly equal societies that sustain the environment and are based on economic democracy. While they might have disagreed on much else, they were both enthusiastic about commons. I think Ostrom would have acknowledged the need for a more macro look at social forces and Marx would have acknowledged the importance too of micro institutional approaches. It is fun to speculate. Clearly though, my feeling is that both a micro, largely Ostrom-inspired view, and a macro, more Marx-influenced view, are useful approaches if we wish to create an ecological, equal and economically democratic future.

Even without picking on a specifically Marxist approach, we can observe that while Elinor Ostrom used historical data, any examination of larger-scale social change does seem absent from her work. A good example is the question of stinting. A stint, as noted previously, is a ration. She discussed how stinting could be used to prevent a tragedy of the commons. In an English context stinting has been defined more precisely as denoting a precise number of animals that can be grazed, this is contrasted with the looser form of rationing where an individual could graze as many animals on the commons as they could maintain over winter. Stints could be turned into a legal property right that could be bought and sold, and seemed to have been part of a transition from a feudal society to a more market based society (Winchester and Straughton 2010).

How, in turn, might Marx and Ostrom be seen as saying similar things and be subject to criticism? I think this is an interesting and important point to discuss.

Both were focused on some kind of political realism. This might seem a strange thing to say, as realism might be seen as the opposite of radicalism. Yet both were interested in what could be achieved within specific social circumstances, rather than in blue sky, utopian thinking. This means in turn that both are broadly materialists. They were concerned not with an idealistic or abstract analysis, but what had a solid, material effect. Marx's use of Hegelian dialectics is a vexed and complex area. What can be said, however, is that he was aware that historical context shaped what was possible. So realism can be applied to both. 'What can we specifically do?' was a question they both asked.

They were also interested in a scientific approach to social change and liberation. The more we understand about society the more likely it will be that we can achieve a better society. Both were critical of simplistic understandings of what social science means. While Marxists have often been accused of an elitist and dogmatic approach to social science, I think Marx was more nuanced. Nevertheless, both Marx and Ostrom, while seeking to use social science, were critical of a simplistic view and respected participants.

I think one way in which both thinkers can be criticised is around the issue of culture. Marx might be perceived as downplaying culture. Ostrom advocated a respect for complexity, and as well as ecology, economic motivations of various sorts, and institutions, she was aware of a cultural element. Norms, which for her were unofficial rules, were a product of culture.

My feeling is that while an institutional analysis and a macro analysis of social forces are necessary, culture needs to be given weight if we are to free ourselves and promote a better society. I am not sure that either Marx or Ostrom fully equip radicals when it comes to cultural politics. Human action is shaped by meaning, and culture shapes us and is shaped by us. We need to discuss the mechanisms of how cultural politics works. A good example is the persistence of nationalism, discussed powerfully and poetically by Benedict Anderson in his book *Imagined Communities* (1991).

Preferences are shaped by culture. This is a fundamental problem for mainstream economics, even if we are rational to some extent and maximise what gives us wellbeing, what determines what give us wellbeing? Nature in a biological sense is also conditioned by human culture. Marx saw social class clearly in material economic terms but material economic interests don't neatly and automatically lead to the social change he suggested.

Much cultural theory – one thinks of Derrida – makes important points but somewhat obscurely. Perhaps we need an Ostrom approach to cultural theory. This is also important in terms of structural influences and individualism. While much cultural theory rejects both methodological individualism and structuralism, the more we know about how culture works, the more we as individuals can see how cultural factors shape us. An Ostrom approach would seek a common language where possible, and seek to aggregate from the very diverse schools of thought that investigate culture, including social psychologists, literary theorists and political philosophers.

Macro structural factors, micro institutional influences and culture cannot in reality be neatly separated, but for research purposes need to be treated one by one so that we can better investigate social reality. The Ostrom approach focuses most specifically on cooperation in the commons, but raises much wider questions. An investigation into culture would enhance our understanding of commons and cooperation but would in a wider way make us able to understand how we are shaped as individuals and how we might, if so desired, reshape ourselves.

Neoliberalism is throwing up huge problems. Inequality and ecological damage, most obviously climate change, are getting worse. Even those who are enthusiastic about neoliberalism, like *The Economist* magazine, are noting that there are huge negative effects. These negative effects are increasingly translated into political discontent which often aids populist right-wing movements who promote isolation, and often blatant hatred. The election of Donald Trump as US President – a billionaire whose supporters include working-class voters whose jobs have been lost or are under threat from globalisation – is one example. Right-wing forces frame problems culturally; the fear of the other is potent and far more powerful than a complex concern with climate change or institutions. It is possible to see a cycle emerging of problems leading to real human suffering being exploited by right-wing politicians, who then make the human suffering worse, but through framing this as a product of migration cement their power more strongly.

Understanding how such framing works and challenging it is vital. Democracy too comes into the mix; in political systems where distant and uncaring bureaucratic elites have power, populism will grow. This isn't entirely a bad thing. An Ostrom approach of promoting self-governance is a good alternative but cultural politics can be used to manipulate people and promote more controlled and repressive societies.

We can derive much wisdom from Elinor Ostrom but this does not preclude having criticism of her work. Certainly, I feel both a class analysis and an analysis of culture are important supplements to her work. This said, she gives us some useful tools for social change.

There are a number of very specific things we can take from Elinor Ostrom's work. If we have a political challenge – for example, fighting to stop open-cast coal mining from despoiling an area of natural beauty – her institutional approach is very useful. It would be possible to pose the issue not just as a principled defence of the environment and the local community, but to ask precisely what it takes to win. While the Institutional Analysis and Development is probably too detailed and complex for local campaigners, it would be useful to map the appropriate institutions. Who has the power? What is the institution that gives permission, what is the composition of the members, what are their choices, what is likely to influence them? Are there other institutions that could block the open-cast coal mine? If, say, the relevant institution is a local planning body, is it possible that a higher body could throw out the plan? What are the means of influence? What resources in terms of media pressure, direct action protest or election campaigns can be used? Elinor promoted a politics of negotiation but her institutionalism also helps us where needed to contest, either defensively or to win more space for radical alternatives.

It is good to ask, what would Elinor do? In doing so we need to be pragmatic, as noted earlier. Some forms of left politics argue that social structures are so powerful that we can make very little change without revolution. Other more centre ground forms of politics assume that in liberal democratic systems principled arguments will win. The Ostrom pragmatism is to keep asking what we can specifically do in a specific context. In terms of much radical politics this moves us from texts to effects, from slogans to analysis.

Often on the left we defend particular courses of action in reference to key texts or key thinkers, an Ostrom approach would see us moving to looking at what works, what is effective, or less so. Texts might be seen as tools for change not sacred documents, again Ostrom's rule of the hammer applies, any text that is useful will not be useful in all situations.

The approach she favoured would be to pose this as a problem, to study alternatives, to see what worked and what didn't work, to tease out some ideas for design features of successful, equal and ecological institutions.

Diversity is very much an Ostrom rule for radicals. It would be possible to establish the best example of a free association of producers, the kind of co-production at the heart of both Marx and Ostrom's thinking. However, one example, or the institutions of one type of body, would not be enough. Human beings are fallible, our knowledge isn't perfect, so if we engage in the construction of a diversity of alternatives, this means that success is more likely than demanding one type.

Fallibility might seem to promote a conservative kind of politics. However, the authoritarian strain of some forms of conservatives falls apart, because if people in general are fallible this does not mean the kings, queens or presidents are less fallible. Our imperfection from an Ostrom perspective does not mean that we are doomed to failure, only that we need to be cautious and gather as much evidence as we can if we are to proceed. Neither does it license a utopian belief in the market. Ostrom as we have seen was not a fundamental critic of the market, she saw much virtue in competition and generally felt that markets were a good way of producing goods and services. However, the Hayekian perspective, that we can leave markets to deal with virtually all areas of human life, is another black box situation. It is an excuse to say either the government will take care of everything or that we can leave everything to the market.

Diversity and co-production show that Ostrom is a thinker for the age of the internet and World Wide Web. Various forms of social sharing, crowd sourcing and peer to peer production increasingly shape the global economy. While she did not spend much time looking at virtual or knowledge commons, her work is very illuminating in the area.

Marx argued that industrialisation was likely to create the pre-conditions for communism, both because it raises the forces of production so we can produce more and because, in a capitalist form, it gives rise to the working class. So far, communism has not emerged in the way that Marx imagined. Hardt and Negri argued that the shift from feudalism also opened up conditions for the liberation of humanity, particularly with the emergence of democratic city states like Florence and the scientific achievements of the renaissance. Again, such hopes for a fully democratic society proved limited. Today, the emergence of the World Wide Web, the vast growth of social media and the potential of 3D printing, might be thought to usher in a world of participatory automated luxury communism. Ostrom is sometimes seen, wrongly, as the prophetess of this kind of commons based society.

Commons are essential and liberating in so many ways. However, an Ostrom approach warns us not to see them as a utopia. Power relations exist within a situation of collective ownership too and commons are not a perfect solution promising universal human liberation. A sharing economy, based on free, touches more and more of our lives. Twenty years ago, who would have thought that much of our access to culture like music, film or knowledge would be free? The present seems utopian if viewed from just a few short years ago. Yet the commons in information and culture has costs. Increasingly, this is dominated by monopolies like Google and Facebook. They don't charge us but they do give our information to others and increasingly are part of government intelligence gathering and corporate control of our data.

The commons is moving into the provision of more and more services in the economy, a good example being the open source trans-portation service Uber. Uber, by allowing drivers and passengers to directly contact each other on the web, has made access to travel far cheaper and easier. However, the owner of this service is a billionaire and traditional taxi drivers are being driven out of business. Ostrom's approach reminds us that any broad institutional structure, whether commons, the state or the market, is likely to be exploited in some way by those with power. Even where power relations give rise to broadly equal outcomes, there are drawbacks to the commons. Ostrom shows that commons are possible but there is a danger that her careful analysis is ignored and her reputation is used to license an uncritical joy and acceptance of any commons. The Marxist approach suggests that in a capitalist society, commons will be made to do the bidding of the ruling class. Ostrom suggests that we need to study actual collective institutions with care and urges us to promote diversity, so we can experiment.

The problem is that political mobilisations depend on the construction of slogans and images. The political economy of a more collective and ecological society demands careful attention to the construction of commons based institutions. We are back, perhaps, to a distinction, that might be derived from a careful reading of Spinoza's work between ideology and science. An ideology mobilises people to make change, a more cautious approach based on extensive research and experiment is needed to make sure that change works. There is a cultural dimension of winning support for the commons and defending the commons. The construction of commons also involves culture, and this seems an element that is hinted at but far from fully explored in Ostrom's work.

Elinor Ostrom's political principles, often lightly held and in the background, are inspiring. We have seen how she put questions of ecology at the centre of her ideas, not at the edge or ignored entirely like most political thinkers. She has a healthy scepticism of blueprints, slogans and top-down rules but didn't see this as an excuse for ignoring the need for broad social equality and feminist politics. She is strong believer in diversity, a value which needs defending in a world where populist politicians increasingly promote uniformity and demonise minorities. Her radical view of democracy is the world turned upside down compared to many theorists, who see politics as separate from everyday life and increasingly about management by elites, with only weak forms of representative democracy. Her ideas about co-production link to all of this, with a notion of making economics democratic and participatory too.

However, these political principles are not, I feel, what is most instructive about Ostrom's work. On the left, and in politics in general, we try to develop principles. This was not her way. She didn't argue, for example, in detail whether deep ecology was better than ecological modernism. She did not undertake any structured investigation of ethics or morality. She was interest in political practice. What she gives radicals is an emphasis on pragmatism. It might be suggested that the more radical one's aims are, the more practical must be the means. Pragmatism has become, with realism, a dirty word on the left. It has generally been associated with the conservation of vested interests, used to argue that it is unrealistic to make a radical different society and powerful vested interests must be accepted and obeyed. The politics of Tony Blair or the Clintons reflects this kind of realism that often makes things worse by supporting powerful elite and corporate interests.

Ostrom's pragmatism is about how to achieve a more cooperative and ecological society. Practical politics for achieving a better future, not practical politics to accumulate power in the hands of a minority, or defence of a corrupt status quo. She emphasised understanding a problem or situation as thoroughly as possible and working out how to achieve material goals in a particular context. Whether it is protecting a rainforest, making a worker-run factory succeed or turning protest like Occupy or the Arab Spring into more than protests, her approach is vital and instructive.

We should remember the many inspiring values that Elinor Ostrom upheld but, above all, we need to keep refining our understanding of how her work can help practical politics. In a world of climate change, other ecological ills, an economic system which is increasingly unequal and where sectarian conflict is on the increase, let's keep asking the question, 'What would Elinor do?'

Bibliography

Acheson, J. (1972) 'Territories of the Lobstermen', *Natural History*, 81: 60–9.

Aligică, P. (2007) *Prophecies of Doom and Scenarios of Progress: Herman Kahn, Julian Simon, and the Prospective Imagination*. London: Continuum.

Aligică, P. (2014) *Institutional Diversity and Political Economy: The Ostroms and Beyond*. Oxford: Oxford University Press.

Aligică, P. and Boettke, P. (2009) *Challenging Institutional Analysis and Development*. London: Routledge.

Aligică, P. and Sabetti, F. (2014) Introduction to Ostrom, E. and Ostrom, V. (2014) *Choice, Rules and Collective Action*. Essex: ECPR Press.

Alinsky, S. (1971) *Rules for Radicals: A Practical Primer for Realistic Radicals*. New York: Vintage Books.

Anderson, B. (1991) *Imagined Communities: Reflections on the Origin and Spread of Nationalism*. London: Verso.

Aristotle (1946) *Politics*. Oxford: Clarendon Press.

Axelrod, R. (1984) *The Evolution of Cooperation*. New York: Basic Books.

Bardhan, P. and Raythe, I. (eds) (2008) *Contested Commons: Conversations Between Economists and Anthropologists*. Oxford: Blackwell.

Beinart, W. (2000) 'African History and Environmental History', *African Affairs*, 99: 269–303.

Benkler, Y. (2005) '"Sharing Nicely": On Shareable Goods and The Emergence of Sharing as a Modality of Economic Production', *The Yale Law Journal*, 114: 273–358.

Benkler, Y. (2006) *The Wealth of Networks*. New Haven and London: Yale University Press.

Bennholdt-Thomsen, V. and Mies, M. (1999) *The Subsistence Perspective: Beyond the Globalised Economy*. London: Zed Press.

Boettke, P. (2012) *Living Economics: Yesterday, Today, and Tomorrow*. Oakland, California: The Independent Institute and Universidad Francisco Marroquin.

Bookchin, M. (1974) *Post-Scarcity Anarchism*. London: Wildwood.

Bookchin, M. (1986) 'Radicalizing Democracy: A Timely Interview with Murray Bookchin', conducted by the editors of Kick It Over. Toronto, Ontario: Northern Lights Press.

Bourdieu, P. (2000) 'Social Space and Symbolic Space' in D. Robbins (ed.) *Pierre Bourdieu, Volume 4*, London: Sage, 3–16.

Caffentzis, G. (2012) 'A Tale of Two Conferences: Globalization, the Crisis of Neoliberalism and Question of the Commons', *Borderlands* 11 (2).

Castiglione, D. (2014) Foreword to Ostrom, E. and Ostrom, V. (2014) *Choice, Rules and Collective Action*. Essex: ECPR Press.

Chakravarty-Kaul, M. (1996) *Common Land and Customary Law*. Oxford: Oxford University Press.

Cole, D. and McGinnis, M.(eds) (2015) *Elinor Ostrom and the Bloomington School of Political Economy: Volume 1, Polycentricity in Public Administration and Political Science*. Lanham, Maryland: Lexington Books.

Cole, D. and McGinnis, M. (eds) (2015) *Elinor Ostrom and the Bloomington School of Political Economy: Volume 2. Resource Governance*. Lanham, Maryland: Lexington Books.

Cronin, B. (2012) *Bloomington Days: Town and Gown in Middle America*. Bloomington, Indiana: AuthorHouse.

Dobson, A. (2000) *Green Political Thought*. London: Routledge.

Dolsak, N. and Ostrom, E. (2003) *The Commons in the New Millennium: Challenges and Adaptations*. Cambridge, MA: MIT Press.

Ecologist. (1992) *Whose Common Future? Reclaiming the Commons*. London: Earthscan.

Elster, J. (1986) *Rational Choice*. Oxford: Blackwell.

Engels, F. (1928) *The Mark*. New York: Labor News Co.

Feyerabend, P. (1975) *Against Method: Outline of an Anarchist Theory of Knowledge*. London: Verso.

Finchett-Maddock, L. (2016) *Protest, Property and the Commons: Performances of Law and Resistance*. New York: Routledge.

Fine, B. (2010) 'Beyond the Tragedy of the Commons: A Discussion of Governing the Commons: The Evolution of Institutions for Collective Action', *Perspectives on Politics*, 8: 583–586.

Fischer, D. (2000) 'Boston Common' in Leuchtenburg, W. *American Places*. New York: Oxford University Press.

Fotos, M. (2013) 'Vincent Ostrom's Revolutionary Science of Association', Unpub. Ostrom Workshop https://ostromworkshop. indiana.edu/pdf/seriespapers/2013s_c/Fotos_paper.pdf

Freire, P. (1968) *Pedagogy of the Oppressed*. New York: Seabury Press.

Hardin, G. (1968) 'The Tragedy of the Commons', *Science*, 162: 1243–1248.

Hardin, G. (1977) 'Lifeboat Ethics: The Case Against Helping the Poor' in Hardin, H. and Baden, J. *Managing the Commons*. San Francisco, California: W.H. Freeman and Company.

Hardt, M. (2010) 'The Commons in Communism' in Douzinas, C. and Žižek, S. (eds) *The Idea of Communism* 131–144. London: Verso.

Hardt, M. and Negri, A. (2000) *Empire*. Cambridge, MA: Harvard University Press.

Hardt, M. and Negri, A. (2009) *Commonwealth*. Cambridge, MA: Harvard University Press.

Harford, T. (2013) 'Do You Believe in Sharing?', *Financial Times*, 30 August.

Harvey, D. (2012) *Rebel Cities. From the Right to the City to Urban Revolution*. London: Verso.

Hayek, F. (1937) 'Economics and Knowledge', *Economica*, 4: 33–54.

Helfrich, S., Kuhlen, R., Sachs, W. and Siefkes, C. (2010) *The Commons: Prosperity by Sharing*. Berlin: Heinrich Böll Foundation.

Hess, C. and Ostrom, E. (2011) *Understanding Knowledge as a Commons*. Cambridge, MA: MIT Press.

Hildyard, N. (2016) *Licensed Larceny*. Manchester: Manchester University Press.

Institutions for Collective Action (n.d.) www.collective-action.info/ glossaries_commons_EnglandWales#S

Korten, D. (1995) *When Corporations Rule the World*. West Hartford, CT: Kumarian Press.

Korten, F. (2010) 'Elinor Ostrom Wins Nobel for Common(s) Sense', *Yes! Magazine*, February.

Krader, L. (ed.) (1972) *The Ethnological Notebooks of Karl Marx*. Amesterdam: Van Gorcum.

Kropotkin, P. (1972) *Mutual Aid: A Factor of Evolution*. New York: New York University.

Leonard, M. (2009) 'Nobel winner Elinor Ostrom is a Gregarious Teacher Who Loves to Solve Problems', *Herald Times*, 6 December.

Lloyd, W. (1833) *Two Lectures on the Checks to Population*. Oxford: Collingwood.

Marx, K. (1976) *Capital* Volume 1. Harmondsworth: Penguin.

May, A.M. and Summerfield, G. (2012) 'Creating a Space where Gender Matters: Elinor Ostrom (1933–2012) talks with Ann Mari May and Gale Summerfield', *Feminist Economics*, 18, 4: 25–37.

Mayr, E. (1982) *The Growth of Biological Thought*. Cambridge, MA: Harvard University Press.

McCarthy, M. (2013) 'Why Half a Million Fritillaries Didn't Make It This Year', http://www.independent.co.uk/environment/nature/naturestudies/why-half-a-million-fritillaries-didn-t-make-it-this-year-8586203.html, *Independent*, 24 April.

McCloskey, D. (1985) *The Rhetoric of Economics*. Madison, WI: University of Wisconsin Press.

McCloskey, D. (1991) 'The Prudent Peasant: New Findings on Open Fields', *Journal of Economic History*, 51: 343–355.

McCloskey, D. (2000) 'Others Things Equal: Free-market Feminism 101', *Eastern Economics Journal*, 26, 3: 363–365.

McGinnis, M. (2011) 'An Introduction to IAD and the Language of the Ostrom Workshop: A Simple Guide to a Complex Framework', *The Policy Studies Journal*, 39, 1: 169–183.

McKean, M. (1982) 'The Japanese Experience with Scarcity: Management of Traditional Common Lands', *Environmental Review*, 6, 2: 63–88.

McKean, M. (1986) 'Management of Traditional Common Lands (Iriaichi) in Japan' in National Research Council, *Proceedings of the Conference on Common Property Resource Management*, Washington, DC: National Academy Press: 533–589.

Montag, W. (1998) Preface to Balibar, E. *Spinoza and Politics*. London: Verso.

Mouffe, C. (2000) *Deliberative Democracy or Agonistic Pluralism*. Vienna: Institute for Advanced Studies.

Neeson, J. (1993) *Commoners: Common Right, Enclosure and Social Change in England, 1700–1820*. Cambridge: Cambridge University Press.

Nelson, G. and Grossberg, L. (1988) *Marxism and the Interpretation of Culture*. Chicago: University of Illinois Press.

Netting, R. (1972) 'Of Men and Meadows: Strategies of Alpine Land Use', *Anthropological Quarterly*, 45: 132–144.

Netting, R. (1976) 'What Alpine Peasants Have in Common: Observations on Communal Tenure in a Swiss Village', *Human Ecology*, 4: 135–146.

Netting, R. (1981) *Balancing on an Alp*. Cambridge: Cambridge University Press.

New, J. (2012) 'Shortly After Death of Wife, Vincent Ostrom Dies', *Indiana Daily Student*, 2 July.

Nobel.org (2009) 'Elinor Ostrom – The Facts' www.nobelprize.org/nobel_prizes/economic-sciences/laureates/2009/ostrom-facts.html

Olson, M. (1965) *The Logic of Collective Action: Public Goods and the Theory of Groups*. Cambridge, MA: Harvard University Press.

Ostrom, E. (1990) *Governing the Commons: The Evolution of Institutions for Collective Action*. Cambridge: Cambridge University Press.

Ostrom, E. (1996) 'Crossing the Great Divide: Coproduction, Synergy and Development', *World Development*, 24, 6: 1073–1087.

Ostrom, E. (1998) 'A Behavioral Approach to the Rational Choice Theory of Collective Action', *American Political Science Review* 92, 1: 1–22.

Ostrom, E. (1999) 'Institutional Rational Choice: An Assessment of the IAD Framework', in Sabatier, P. (ed.) *Theories of the Policy Process*. Boulder, CO: Westview Press.

Ostrom, E. (2003) 'Towards a Behavioral Theory Linking Trust, Reciprocity and Reputation', in Ostrom, E. and Walker, J. *Trust and Reciprocity: Interdisciplinary Lessons from Experimental Research*. New York: Russell Sage Foundation.

Ostrom, E. (2004) 'The Ten Most Important Books', *Tidskriftet Politik*, 4, 7: 36–48.

Ostrom, E. (2005) *Understanding Institutional Diversity*. Princeton, NJ.: Princeton University Press.

Ostrom, E. (2007) 'Engaging Impossibilities and Possibilities', In Basu, K. and Kanbur, R. (eds) *Arguments for a Better World: Essays in Honor of Amartya Sen* volume 2. New York: Oxford University Press.

Ostrom, E. (2008) 'Crafting rules to sustain resources', *The American Academy of Political and Social Science*. www.aapss.org/news/crafting-rules-to-sustain-resources/

Ostrom, E. (2009a) A General Framework for Analyzing Sustainability of Social-Ecological Systems', *Science*, 325: 419–422.

Ostrom, E. (2009b) 'Big Think Interview with Elinor Ostrom', *Big Think*, 14 November. http://bigthink.com/videos/big-think-interview-with-elinor-ostrom

Ostrom, E. (2010a) 'Beyond Markets and States: Polycentric Governance of Complex Economic Systems', *American Economic Review*, 100, 3: 641–672.

Ostrom, E. (2010b) 'A Long Polycentric Journey', *Annual Review of Political Science*, 13, 1–23.

Ostrom, E. (2010c) 'Institutional Analysis', in Crothers, C. *Historical Developments and Theoretical Approaches in Sociology/Social Theory*. Oxford: Eolss Publishers.

Ostrom, E. (2010d) 'An interview with Elinor Ostrom', *Annual Reviews Conversations*, www.annualreviews.org/userimages/ContentEditor/1326999553977/ElinorOstromTranscript.pdf

Ostrom, E. (2011) *Guest Introduction. Grassroots Economic Organizing (GEO) Newsletter, Volume 2, Issue 9.* http://geo.coop/node/647

Ostrom, E. (2012) 'Green from the Grassroots', Project Syndicate. 12 June. www.project-syndicate.org/commentary/green-from-the-grassroots

Ostrom, E. (2014) 'A polycentric approach for coping with climate change', *Annals of Economics and Finance*, 15, 1: 71–108.

Ostrom, E., Chang, C., Pennington, M. and Tarko, V. (2012) *The Future of the Commons*. London: Institute of Economic Affairs.

Ostrom, E., Gardner, R. and Walker, J. (1994) *Rules, Games, and Common Pool Resources*. Ann Arbor, MI: University of Michigan Press.

Ostrom, E. and Ostrom, V. (2014) *Choice, Rules and Collective Action*. Essex: ECPR Press.

Ostrom, V. (1953) *Water and Politics: A Study of Water Policies and Administration in the Development of Los Angeles*. Los Angeles: The Haynes Foundation.

Ostrom, V. (1969) *Organization* (unpublished). http://dlc.dlib. indiana.edu/dlc/bitstream/handle/10535/4377/VOOR69AA. pdf?sequence=1&isAllowed=y

Ostrom, V. (1980) 'Artisanship and Artifact', *Public Administration Review* 40,4: 309–317.

Ostrom, V. (1991) *The Meaning of American Federalism: Constituting a Self-Governing Society*. San Francisco: Institute for Contemporary Studies Press.

Ostrom, V. (1997) *The Meaning of Democracy and the Vulnerability of Democracies: A Response to Tocqueville's Challenge*. Ann Arbor, MI: University of Michigan Press.

Ostrom, V., Tiebout, C. and Warren, R. (1961) 'The Organization of Government in Metropolitan Areas: A Theoretical Inquiry', *American Political Science Review*, 55, 831–842.

Parekh, B. (2015) *Marx's Theory of Ideology*. London: Routledge.

Polski, M. and Ostrom, E. (1999) *An Institutional Framework for Policy Analysis and Design*. Workshop in Political Theory and Policy Analysis Working Paper W98–27. Virginia: George Mason University.

Rose, C. (1994) *Property and Persuasion: Essays on the History, Theory and Rhetoric of Ownership*. Boulder, CO: Westview Press.

Rose, C. (2003) 'Romans, Roads and Romantic Creators: Traditions of Public Property in the Information Age', *Law and Contemporary Problems*, 66: 89–110.

Schlüter, A. and Madrigal, R. (2012) 'The SES Framework in a Marine Setting: Methodological Lessons', *Rationality, Markets and Morals*, 3: 158–179.

Sen, A. (1990) 'More Than 100 Million Women Are Missing', *New York Review of Books*, 20 December.

Simon, H. A. (1955). 'A behavioral model of rational choice'. *The Quarterly Journal of Economics*, 69(1), 99–118.

Simon, J. (1981) *The Ultimate Resource*. Princeton, NJ: Princeton University Press.

Smith, A. (2006) *The Theory of Moral Sentiments*. New York: Dover.

Spiegel Online (2009) 'Nobel Laureate Elinor Ostrom: Climate Rules Set from the Top Are Not Enough'. www.spiegel.de/international/world/nobel-laureate-elinor-ostrom-climate-rules-set-from-the-top-are-not-enough-a-667495.html

Spinoza, B. (1951) *A Theologico-Political Treatise and a Political Treatise*. New York: Dover.

Spivak, G. (1988) 'Can the Subaltern Speak?', in Nelson, G. and Grossberg, L. (eds) *Marxism and the Interpretation of Culture*. London: Macmillan.

Sullivan, M. (2011) '10 Questions for UCLA's Nobel Prize winning economist Elinor Ostrom', *UCLA Today*.

Tarko, V. (2016) *Elinor Ostrom: An Intellectual Biography*. Lanham, Maryland: Rowland and Littlefield.

Tocqueville, A. (1994) *Democracy in America*. New York: Alfred A. Knopf.

Von Mises, L. (2008) *Human Action*. New York: Laissez Faire Books.

Von Neumann, J. and Morgenstern, O. (1944) *Theory of Games and Economic Behavior*. Princeton, NJ: Princeton University Press.

Walljasper, J. (2014) The Story of Vincent and Elinor Ostrom. On the Commons. www.onthecommons.org

Wall, D. (2014a) *The Sustainable Economics of Elinor Ostrom*. London: Routledge.

Wall, D. (2014b) *The Commons in History*. Cambridge, MA: MIT Press.

Wainwright H. (2016) 'A New Politics From the Left?', *Open Democracy*/ISA RC-47: Open Movements, 19 May. https://opendemocracy.net/hilary-wainwright/new-politics-from-left

Waring, M. (1989) *If Women Counted: A New Feminist Economics*. London: Macmillan.

Winchester, A. and Straughton, E. (2010) 'Stints and Sustainability: Managing stock levels on common land in England, c.1600–2006', *Agricultural History Review*, 58, 1: 30–48.

RESOURCES FOR CHANGE

The Ostrom Workshop can be found at http://ostromworkshop. indiana.edu/home.php

Digital Library of the Commons Repository is an online library of thousands of articles and documents about commons, a fantastic resource, which was put together by Elinor and Vincent: http://dlc. dlib.indiana.edu/dlc/

The International Journal of the Commons is an open source academic journal initiated by the Ostroms www.thecommonsjournal.org

There are a huge number of commons sites and campaigns on the internet including On the Commons www.onthecommons.org

Index